THE MEANING OF RITUAL

The Meaning of Ritual

by
Leonel L. Mitchell

PAULIST PRESS
New York/Ramsey/Toronto

Library of Congress
Catalog Card Number: 77-78215

ISBN: 0-8091-2035-6

Published by Paulist Press
Editorial Office: 1865 Broadway, New York, N.Y. 10023
Business Office: 545 Island Road, Ramsey, N.J. 07446

Printed and bound in the
United States of America

Contents

Preface

My purpose in this book is to examine human ritual, and especially Western Christian ritual, to see what place it holds in human life, and whether it can continue to hold that place today. It is not addressed to the specialist but to the general reader and seeks to place a study of liturgical origins and meaning in the wider context of human ritual activity.

This material was originally developed in connection with an introductory undergraduate course I have been teaching at the University of Notre Dame; I am indebted to many classes of students who served as the sounding board against whom I tried to make my ideas on this subject resonate. Their reactions have been most helpful in giving me a "feel" for where many young men and women are today regarding ritual worship.

Introduction

It is frequently suggested today that we have lost our ability to deal with ritual, that symbols no longer speak to us. I do not believe that is true. I do think we have seen that certain symbols, specifically religious symbols, which were filled with meaning for people of an earlier age, no longer have any meaning for us, and we either know or strongly suspect that they have no meaning for some of those who use them.

The anthropologist Mary Douglas entitled the first chapter of her book *Natural Symbols*[1] "Away from Ritual" and spoke of the "explicit rejection of rituals as such" and of "a revolt against formalism, even against form"[2] as characteristic of the present. The liturgist Romano Guardini asked in 1964, "Would it not be better to admit that man in this industrial and scientific age, with its new sociological structure, is no longer capable of a liturgical act?"[3] The word "ritual" itself has for many, even for most people, a negative connotation. They associate it with "vain repetition," with meaningless activity, with formalism, and with "going through the motions." Many sociologists, for example, describe as a ritualist "one who performs external gestures without inner commitment to the ideas being expressed."[4]

Obviously there is very little to be said in favor of this sort of ritualism. It undoubtedly serves a useful function in the many social rituals which smooth over our encounters with one another, such as the greeting,

"How are you?" which is not really a question. I am not really scandalized that the gentleman who extends his hand and mutters, "Pleased to meet you," is in fact not particularly pleased, but when the reality symbolized by the external gesture has more significance, I feel betrayed when I realize that the actor is truly uncommitted to the values implied in his action. The preacher who says, "I believe," and does not, like the lover who says, "I love," and does not, is a fraud and a betrayer, especially when he follows up his profession of faith with appropriate symbolic action, such as making love or making eucharist. We have every right to object if the commitment implied in word and action is absent.

On the other hand, as far as I know, no one has been so foolish as to suggest that since the powerful ritual acts of sexual relationship frequently do not carry the full weight of meaning which they should and are often used by the unscrupulous as means of manipulating other people, they should be abandoned by human beings in favor of some more meaningful form of activity. Unfortunately, this is precisely the suggestion that is frequently made in the case of the powerful ritual acts of religious relationship.

Ritual As a Neutral Term

What I am trying to suggest is that there is another meaning of "ritual," one that does not have negative connotations, one in which there is commitment to the inner reality symbolized by external gesture. Anthropologists and historians of religion, for example, use the word "ritual" in a completely neutral sense to mean an agreed upon pattern of movement. Ritual, in this sense, has been described at its most basic level as two children avoiding the cracks in the sidewalk.[5] It makes no reference to the inner commitment or non-commitment of the actors; it simply describes what they do. In this sense it is not even necessarily a religious word. It may refer to the actions of the spectators at a football game, to the blowing out of candles on a birthday cake, to a champagne toast and a kiss at the beginning of the New Year, or to the distribution of keys to the executive washroom, or the placement of party functionaries in the reviewing stand in Red Square for the May Day parade.

As the word stands in the title of this book it is used in this neutral sense as a general word for corporate symbolic activity. Normally, we shall be speaking of religious ritual, the activity in which people engage when they worship. That in itself presents another difficulty, for worship is extraordinarily difficult to explain. The contemporary theologian Marianne Micks appropriately compares it to love:

> People who worship and people who love generally suppose that they know what they are doing. They assume that other people are doing something similar under the same name. But worship, like love, is a curiously difficult activity to talk about. If one asks worshipers, "What, precisely, is it that you are doing?" no one can say very clearly.[6]

The situation is even worse if we ask, "Why, precisely, are you doing it?" We are almost driven to respond, "If you have to ask, you wouldn't understand if I explained it." But "What?" and "Why?" are precisely the questions we must ask and attempt to answer.

Obviously religious ritual, like any other ritual, can become an empty form. People can, and do "go through the motions." There is today a tremendous and totally justified reaction against this form of mumbo-jumbo. It is worse than useless. It is evil, even demonic.

The Direction of Ritual Today

Religious ritual is not always empty of meaning, however, and Christianity is not alone among world religions in seeing external actions as the necessary means of conveying and expressing interior realities. Love, whether of God or of the girl next door, is all but impossible to express except through outward symbolic action, that is, through ritual acts. The same is true of friendship, respect, or, for that matter, hatred or contempt. We kiss, shake hands, shake our fist, turn our backs. These are ritual actions. They are all around us in our daily lives. We cannot avoid them. The question of ritual today is not, "Can we do without it?" Obviously, we cannot, even if we want to. It is rather, "Can we use the religious rituals we have inherited from the past?"

For many people the answer to this question is a resounding, if reluctant "No!" They consider religious ritual to be something man has outgrown. It was probably necessary, they believe, for primitive man in a pre-scientific, pre-modern world, but it fulfills no useful function in the contemporary world. It is a survival with which we may freely dispense. Even if they are willing to follow Peter Berger in making a place for the supernatural in their lives,[7] there does not really seem to be a place for ritual. Against this view Margaret Mead has spoken out forcefully:

> I do not think ritual can be relegated to the past— to antiquity, to barbarism, or to the life of early man. Ritual is an exceedingly important part of all culture, all the cultures we know about and, hopefully, all cultures that we will know about.[8]

Dr. Mead goes on to explain why she thinks that ritual holds such an important place in culture:

> It is a major function of ritual in human society to permit those who are appropriately gifted to work together on forms that will be available to everyone, including those who are, as one might say, religiously gifted but who lack the power to express their experience in forms that are available to others . . . It is on ritual forms that the imagination of each generation feeds.[9]

For us, as much as for primitive man, it is a good ritual system which will enable us to find meaning in the universe and in our own lives. It seems, in fact, that it is just such a lack of meaning which characterizes much of contemporary society, and it is not impossible that it is the rejection of ritual which has denied us access to this meaning.

In a more profound sense, however, we cannot reject ritual. We can only reject specific traditional rituals by substituting new and different rituals for them. Mircea Eliade, the historian of religions, calls symbolic thinking "consubstantial with human existence." "It comes," he says, "before language and discursive reason."[10] We may disguise, mutilate, or degrade the symbols which are the very substance of human spiritual life, but we cannot rid ourselves of them, and ritual, as we have already said, is nothing more than corporate symbolic action.

People have, of course, attempted to do without ritual in worship. The early Quakers rejected the traditional Christian ritual system, and expressed their rejection by wearing their hats in church, sitting throughout the "meeting" for worship, and using no fixed forms of prayer, but breaking silence only at the prompting of the Spirit. This very rejection was itself a new ritual system expressing symbolically their break with the traditional liturgical Church and their willingness to be led by the inner light of the Holy Spirit.

In the present generation many who reject traditional Christian ritual have made place in their lives for all kinds of exotic Oriental religious rituals. College students who would consider wearing a cassock and chanting the psalms to Gregorian chants the height of medieval superstition do not hesitate to appear in public in saffron robes, sit in uncomfortable positions and chant mantras in unknown languages. Zen, Hare Krishna, and Transcendental Meditation, to say nothing of astrology, satanism, and black magic, are openly practiced in America today, chiefly but by no means exclusively on college campuses. It is worth considering the possibility that it is the rejection and impoverishment of ritual and symbol in Western culture, Christian and otherwise, which has led so many to seek to experience the ecstasy to which the true knowledge of the meaning of life leads in other cultures and life styles.[11]

The impoverishment of which I speak is that which looks at the natural world and sees only a collection of physical phenomena. Thomas Aquinas thought he could look at the created universe and prove the existence of God. Jesus ben Sirach wrote, "Consider the rainbow, and praise him who made it."[12] Primitive man in traditional societies sees his world as sacred, as filled with what Eliade calls hierophanies, that is, manifestations of the sacred.[13] We do not see the world that way, unless we are poets or artists. A sunset does not always inspire us to sing, "Benedicite omnia opera Domini Domino! Let all the works of the Lord bless the Lord!" although it is pointed out with some justice by theologians like Robert Capon and Alexander Schmemann that it would be most natural to do so.[14] We live in a dead world of physical phenomena which points to nothing beyond itself.

This picture is, I hope, somewhat overdrawn. Even the most devoted observer of physical phenomena will recognize that describing beauty in terms of chemical makeup, geometric configuration, physical mass, and frequencies of light waves is hopelessly inadequate. And it is with this recognition that there is more to life than its measurable phenomena that our study of the meaning of ritual must begin.

NOTES

1. Mary Douglas, *Natural Symbols* (New York: Random House, 1970, 1973). References are to the Vintage Books edition of October 1973.

2. Douglas, *Symbols*, p. 19.

3. "A Letter from Romano Guardini," *Herder Correspondence* (August 1964), p. 239.

4. Douglas, *Symbols*, p. 20.

5. Philip Wheelwright, *The Burning Fountain*, quoted

in Marianne Micks, *The Future Present* (New York: Seabury, 1970), p. 20.

6. Micks, *Future*, p. ix.

7. Cf. Peter Berger, *A Rumor of Angels* (Garden City, NY: Doubleday, 1970), especially ch. 1, "The Alleged Demise of the Supernatural."

8. Margaret Mead, "Ritual Expression of the Cosmic Sense," *Worship* 40 (1966), p. 67.

9. Mead, "Ritual," p. 69.

10. Mircea Eliade, *Images and Symbols* (New York: Sheed and Ward, 1969), p. 12.

11. Berger, *Rumor*, p. 28.

12. Ecclesiasticus 43:11.

13. Mircea Eliade, *The Sacred and the Profane* (New York: Harcourt, Brace, and World, 1959), p. 11.

14. Robert F. Capon, *An Offering of Uncles* (New York: Sheed and Ward, 1967); Alexander Schmemann, *For the Life of the World* (Crestwood, N.Y.: St.Vladimir's Seminary Press, 1973).

1

The Beginnings of Ritual Worship

Evelyn Underhill has given what is probably the best general definition of worship. She calls it "the response of the creature to the Eternal."[1] It is the recognition that there are forces or powers greater than we in the world and the expression of our wish to relate to them.

The Earliest Evidence

It should not seem strange to Christians whose highest form of worship is a sacred meal, the Lord's Supper, to discover that some of the oldest rituals of which we have any evidence are those connected with the obtaining and eating of food.[2] This evidence dates from the third interglacial period (approximately 180,000 to 120,000 B.C.) and was left by the prehistoric hunters of cave bears in Alpine caves nearly 8,000 feet above sea level. Their preservation is due to the return of the ice, which buried them under a thick layer of earth before it retreated.[3]

According to Johannes Maringer, the most impressive example of these remains is the Drachenloch in the eastern part of the Swiss Alps.[4] He believes the cave

1

contains clear evidence of ritual activity in connection with the hunting of cave bears. It contains a number of undamaged bear skulls in an altar-like stone chest, and others set in protected niches. The bones were unbroken, indicating that the brain and the bone marrow, considered to be delicacies, had not been removed. Maringer gives this explanation:

> It is quite clear from the finds that the center of the ritual was not the head or skull or long bones in themselves, but those prized delicacies of all hunters—the brain and marrow. These precious parts of the animal were offered to the divine dispenser of hunting fortune in token of thanks for benefits received and to entreat success in future expeditions. The frequent orientation of the remains toward the exit may well mean that this deity was believed to abide somewhere in the universe beyond the cave.[5]

We do not, of course, know what sort of rituals these hunters of the middle Paleolithic Age practiced in front of or within their caves. Did they, perhaps, invoke the protection of a "master of the animals" before setting out on a hunt, and promise him a portion of their victim? The slaying of an animal as large as a cave bear must have been the result of tremendous courage and skill on the part of hunters who followed their prey over 8,000 feet up into the Alps, combined with a considerable measure of luck. Were their rites thanks-offerings for a successful hunt, or designed to secure a supply of game for future hunting? We can only guess. Maringer looks for clues in the present practice of primitive arctic hunters, who similarly preserve the skulls and long-bones of their game and consider the brain and marrow to be a sacrifice to the "dispenser of hunting fortune."[6]

Prehistoric Cave Paintings

The end of the interglacial period brought with it the emergence of a new type of man in Europe, usually referred to as the Cro-Magnon, who has left us most remarkable evidence of his presence in the murals that he painted on the walls of his caves. The first examples were found in 1902, but it was the discovery of the great cave of Lascaux in France in 1940 that brought Ice Age art to the attention of the world. It is generally recognized that this age ended approximately 10,000 B.C. There is less agreement as to its length, although a reasonable estimate would date the art between 30,000 and 10,000 B.C.[7]

The drawings in the caves are so placed that they cannot be seen without the greatest difficulty: at the end of long winding tunnels where there is no natural light. Often they are drawn or painted one on top of another. Most of the paintings are of large animals, such as bear, reindeer, elk, bison, horses, or mammoths, either mating, giving birth, or at the point of death. The general view of these paintings is that they are of ritual significance, connected in some way with the hunting of the animals themselves.

The Ice Age hunter, even more than the modern sportsman, was strangely bound to the prey he hunted, for to him, if the game supply gave out, it meant not a ruined vacation, but starvation and death. He cared desperately that the mammoth mated in season and produced a good supply of offspring. It was important to him that he be able to kill them, and eat and share in their great strength—not only symbolically, but actually, for he ate the meat, clothed himself with the hide, and fashioned tools from the bones.

The Meaning of the Paintings

It has sometimes been suggested that the purpose of the paintings was the practice of sympathetic magic, that is, to enable the cavemen to kill the beasts, much as practitioners of voodoo stick pins in a doll. By symbolizing the death of the beast in a wall painting, the hunter would gain control over it. In the same way, by painting the mating of elk, or the birth of a bison, the animals were made to reproduce. Maringer himself refers to the rites of the painters as magic, but concedes that the sacrifices of the earlier bear hunters provide the religious background for the magic. "It is quite possible," he admits, "that most of the late ice-age hunters' ritual practices that are referred to as 'magical' were in fact—like most of those of primitive hunting people today—genuinely religious."[8]

Adolf Jensen, author of *Myth and Cult among Primitive Peoples* and a distinguished authority on primitive religion, writes:

> There is no justification for representing prehistoric rock paintings as "magical art," as we see it done with great regularity. . . . If ethnological findings are to explain prehistoric phenomena, only proven facts and not dubious conjectures should be admitted. Such data can be found among some archaic peoples who even today draw

rock pictures. Here everything affirms that the practices are cultic acts performed in genuinely religious spirit. . . . All of this speaks against the magical origin of prehistoric painting.[9]

Another approach is to note the location of the paintings. They are barely accessible, and must have been almost totally invisible to both men and beasts before the invention of modern artificial light. If they were intended for sympathetic magic, you would expect to find them in the open, where they might directly influence the animals, as we find in the example of sympathetic magic in Genesis 30.

Among the animal figures in the caves there are some of human beings dressed as animals. The most extraordinary is in the deepest part of the Trois Frères in southern France and is usually called "the great sorcerer." His figure, about twelve feet above the floor of the cave, dominates an entire chamber of animal paintings. He has the antlered head of a deer, the face of an owl, the pointed ears of a wolf, the beard of a chamois, bearlike paws, and a horse's tail. The legs alone are human, and the figure is dancing.[10] These figures probably do not really represent human beings, but a divine being, a "master of the animals" who gives success in hunting. In the Trois Frères cave there is a narrow spiral passage that would have permitted a "sorcerer" or "priest" to stand in front of the image of the "great sorcerer" and officiate at rites designed to ensure success in hunting and animal fertility.

It is possible that the "great sorcerer" is the "god" to whom the rites performed in the caves were addressed, and that it was for his eyes that the paintings were made.[11] It has also been suggested that the paint-

ings were for the benefit of the Earth itself, the Great
Mother from whom all life springs.[12]

The "religious" explanation of the paintings sees
them as acts of worship, thanksgiving to the source of
life for the abundant supply of game, or requests for a
more abundant supply, and either thanksgiving for permission to kill the game or a request for that permission. The actual hunting of the game, whether we take
the "religious" or the "magical" view, is then surrounded by rituals, of which the climax is the killing of the
beast, followed by the feast on the meat—a feast in
which the power or powers who assisted in the kill
might claim a share. It is almost certain that the ritual
form we call sacrifice developed from the ritualized
hunt. It is a basic ritual action performed by men as
part of their dawning awareness of the ecology of their
world.

A Pygmy Hunting Ritual

While we do not know exactly what form the rituals of the cave painters took, we can examine a twentieth-century anthropologist's description of what a
modern Stone Age culture did in one instance. Leo
Frobenius led an expedition to Equatorial Africa in
1905 and described a hunting ritual performed by the
pygmies.[13]

The events unfolded in this way. Frobenius
requested four pygmies who were travelling with him to
kill him an antelope for food. They assured him that it
was impossible that day since no preparations had been
made, but that they would make the necessary preparations and hunt the following day. That morning before

sunrise they cleared and smoothed a space at the top of a hill. On the cleared ground one of them drew a three-foot-long antelope, while all recited some ritual formula. Then all waited in silence for the sunrise. As the rays of the sun fell on the drawing, the woman in the group cried out and raised her hands to the sun, while one of the men shot an arrow into the neck of the drawing. The woman continued to cry out and the men went off into the bush with their weapons. That afternoon the hunters returned with an antelope with an arrow through its jugular vein. The next morning before sunrise the pygmies returned to the hilltop with some tufts of antelope hair and a bowl of its blood. Using the hair as brushes they smeared the drawing with the blood, removed the arrow and erased the drawing.

Jensen reminds us[14] that we really know almost as little about this rite as we do about the prehistoric cave paintings, since we do not know the myth that corresponds to the rite. But we can observe certain things. The hunting itself is a part of a ritual. In the final act of the ritual, the blood, which symbolizes the sacred life of the animal, is returned to the Earth, from which it came. Certainly the sun is central to the ritual. It may, perhaps, symbolize the sky-father whose union with the earth-mother produces life, and whose permission is needed before life can be taken.

Whatever the exact meaning of this ritual, it is obvious that the slaying of the animal was a part of a rite. Killing without performing the ritual was unthinkable to the pygmies, as apparently it was generally to primitive man. The taking of life was serious business, and it was hedged about with ritual prescriptions, the purpose of which was to give the hunter permission to kill his prey and to assure the replenishment of the supply of game. We appear to be dealing with the basic ritual type that is called "sacrifice," or at least with something very like it.

Rites of Initiation

A second basic ritual type is initiation. If the first theme had to do with the hunt and food, this one has to do with the hunter. Hunting a large animal with a spear, a stone axe, or a bow and arrow is not a job for an individual. It is a community project. It takes a band of hunters to kill a mammoth. Each hunter quite literally trusts his life to his fellows. He has therefore a high stake in both their loyalty and their competence. If the man next to me turns and runs, whether through cowardice or lack of ability, I am very likely to be killed. I want to know who my fellow hunters are.

This is why cultures develop initiatory rituals, ceremonies and ordeals to make men out of boys. It is a way to be sure of their loyalty and ability.

The best general definition of initiation is that given by the historian of religions, Mircea Eliade:

The term initiation in the most general sense denotes a body of rites and oral teachings whose purpose is to produce a decisive alteration in the religious and social status of the person to be initiated. In philosophical terms, initiation is equivalent to a basic change in existential condition; the novice emerges from the ordeal endowed with a totally different being from that which he possessed before his initiation; he has become *another*.[15]

This definition applies to a great variety of rites in both ancient and modern times. In general, rites of this type may be recognized as having three basic parts, which are not always equally important or equally elaborated. These are rites of separation, rites of transition (or liminal rites), and rites of incorporation.[16]

In the modern world this structure is preserved not only in rites called initiations, such as initiations into religious or fraternal societies, but in forms for becoming a naturalized citizen, in formal marriage customs, in monastic professions, and in ordination rites. In a formal marriage, the engagement, sometimes in itself a complex ceremonial occasion involving banquets, ritual toasts, and public proclamation, is the rite of separation, separating the couple from the world of "singles" who are available for dates, parties, etc. The period of the engagement is an almost archetypal liminal state. The couple are neither married nor single. The status is filled with tension, frustration, and confusion. It is a special relationship in which not only the couple themselves but society in general expect a particular sort of activity. Finally, the marriage itself is the rite of incorporation, the entry into the new state, and its announcement to society. In the case of the woman it even involves the adoption of a new name.

In a more formal period the rite could be further broken down, so that the marriage itself would exhibit the threefold division. The marriage service would be a rite of separation, clearly separating the engaged couple from all others. The honeymoon becomes a liminal state in which they learn how to be husband and wife, and the final act of incorporation is the "at home" when they receive their friends in their new home and new status as Mr. and Mrs. So-and-so.

In primitive societies the initiation rites that make a child an adult member of the tribe are of primary importance. Eliade describes this initiation as introducing the candidate into the human community and into the world of spiritual and cultural values. "In modern terms," he writes, "we could say that initiation puts an end to the natural man and introduces the novice to culture."[17] The culture, however, is not thought of as being man-made, but is the gift of divine beings.

It is at least possible that initiation rituals go back to the period of the Ice Age hunters. Certainly the most primitive initiation rites that survive have to do with the initiation of men into the band of hunters. It is at least possible that the great chambers decorated with the pictures of animals we have described were used as sites for initiation ceremonies. A bull-roarer remarkably similar to those used by Australian aborigines in their initiation rites has been found in the Magdalenian layer (about 10,000 B.C.) of a French cave.[18] Bull-roarers are perforated oval objects attached to a cord that make a humming noise when whirled. The Australian aborigines call them the voice of their god.

As long as men and women had different social and religious roles, there were different initiation rites for the two sexes. They were, in fact, initiated into different societies to do different things. This need not imply male superiority, but only that the sex roles were different and required different initiations. We have seen evidence of the concern of the Ice Age hunter with animal fertility. He was no less concerned with the increase of his own species, or at least his own tribe, and there is some evidence of a fertility cult and the worship of a "Mother Goddess."[19]

Rites for Boys

A typical boys' initiation rite as performed in a primitive or archaic society today would follow this pattern.[20] First the "sacred ground," the site where the initiates will be isolated during their liminal period, is prepared. This may take the form of a ceremonial house, or a place apart from the village. Frequently it includes one or more sacred circles and is usually decorated with images, sacred signs, or pictures. It is a microcosm, an *imago mundi*; a model of the real, or sacred, world.

The initiation itself begins with a rite of separation, in which the boys are separated from their mothers and the life of childhood so that they may become men and share henceforth in that new life. Childish things are completely put away. The break is often dramatic and violent. The boys might be seated in a circle around a fire with their mothers placed behind them and covered with blankets or branches. The men approach from the sacred ground, whirling bull-roarers, beating the ground with rods, and throwing burning sticks. The women and children are forbidden to peek under pain of death. The men seize the boys and carry them off to the sacred ground. There they are made to lie on the ground and are covered with branches.

The mothers believe their sons will be killed, and indeed they never do get their little boys back. The boys themselves are completely terrorized. They are placed in unfamiliar surroundings, in the dark, and often told they will be devoured by divine beings. The men who seize them are often masked, and the entire ritual is designed to fill them with forebodings of death. It is indeed a ritual death. Their old lives as children are over and they are dead, buried in the dark under the branches, waiting to be reborn as men.

The second stage of the rite is the transition, or liminal period. During it the boys are kept isolated in the sacred ground. They may be required to undergo certain ordeals during this period. It is also during this period that the old initiates, the spiritual masters, instruct the novices in the tribal culture. This is usually done in mythic terms; that is, the various skills and pieces of knowledge they need are explained as gifts of the gods, as the divine learning they have taught us. The matters explained to the initiates are usually hunting and food gathering, the understanding of the meaning of death, and the culture's understanding of sexuality. Much of this material is oral lore, but some of it may be skills that need to be acquired. This period is sometimes substantial in length, or the initiation may take place in stages to give the initiates time to gain the requisite skills.

During this period, or at its close, certain operations are usually performed on the initiate. Often the boys are circumcised, or a tooth is knocked out. Sometimes they are tattooed or scarred. This is the mark of their initiation that identifies them as adult male members of their society.

Finally the initiates, marked as men, are incorporated into the tribe. In some places they are painted white to resemble ghosts—a clear indication that this is indeed a resurrection after ritual death. The marks of their initiation separate them from the noninitiates. The final act is a religious rite, frequently concluding with the sharing of a meal as a rite of incorporation. The initiates are no longer children but men, and are expected to take a man's part in the acquisition of food.

The initiates who are reborn as men in these rites are integrated into the adult community, which is thereby regenerated and renewed. The rites are therefore central not only to the individual initiates but to the entire culture. In many languages the word for human being is the same as that for an initiated member of the tribe. In a real sense, only the initiates are treated as human beings, for the uninitiated are not really considered to be people. Cultures as civilized as Classical Greece were able to practice the exposing of unwanted children, since they did not really consider them people until the father had performed the necessary rites. Even today our culture tends to treat "natives" or "gooks" or those not a part of Western civilization as non-people.

Rites for Girls

We know less about girls' initiations. Probably this is because most of the researchers have been men from whom women would carefully conceal the nature of their rites. The ceremonies tend to be less complex, but to follow the same general lines.[21] Girls, however, are initiated individually. The onset of menstruation marks the break with childhood, and the girl is immediately segregated from the rest of society. The period of this segregation varies from a few days to several years, so that eventually the girls in some places do form a group and their initiation is completed collectively.

During their transition period they are normally kept in the dark and may actually be forbidden to see the sun. During this period they are taught by the older women. They learn ritual songs, dances, and those skills appropriate to women in the culture. Among these, spinning and weaving are important and are often given cosmological meaning as the spinning and weaving of Time and Destiny. The core of the initiation appears to revolve around the sacrality of women and their role as creators of life. In cultures that practice agriculture, planting seed and growing crops are often among the mysteries dependent upon the women's role. Eliade comments:

> For boys, initiation represents an introduction to a world that is not immediate—the world of spirit and culture. For girls, on the contrary, initiation involves a series of revelations concerning the secret meaning of a phenomenon that is apparently natural—the visible sign of their sexual maturity.[22]

The ceremonial normally ends with a ritual bath after which the girl is solemnly *shown* to the community as an adult. This is a proclamation that the mystery has been accomplished, and the initiate is ready to assume her place as a woman in society.

In addition to these initiation rites there are often also degrees of higher initiation. Marriage is an initiation ritual; so frequently is the birth of a first child. Funeral rites are formed on the pattern of initiation rites to help the dead into the next world. The rites of separation are performed here in the expectation that, after an appropriate transition period, the rites of incorporation will welcome them into the next world. There are also shamanistic initiations. All of these forms still exist in the higher religions such as Christianity. Baptism, marriage, and ordination are Christian initiatory rites built on these primitive bases.

Levels of Meaning

All of these primitive rituals, and the images and symbols from which they are built are multivalent; that is, they have several meanings at once. These meanings build one on another, and if the higher levels of meaning come to dominate, the others nonetheless remain and inform the whole. For Christians, for example, the bread and wine of the Eucharist derive their sacramental significance from the institution of Jesus at the Last Supper. This does not destroy, but rather builds upon the natural significance of sharing bread and wine. In the same way baptism derives its Christian meaning from the baptism of Jesus, and our participation in the mystery of his death and resurrection, but it still is an initiatory rite, using the symbol of water and the scenario of ritual death and resurrection. Easter itself celebrates the resurrection of Christ, not the rebirth of flowers in the spring, but we do not hesitate to sing on Easter morning:

Lo, the fair beauty of earth,
from the death of the winter arising!
Every good gift of the year
now with its Master returns.[23]

Each new level of meaning adds to the natural structure, even if it completely overshadows it. Christian ritual, then, springs out of a whole pattern of ritual actions. Historically Christianity is rooted in Judaism so that in one sense Jewish ritual is the root of Christian, but in a larger sense it is rooted in all ritual. There are certain great images and symbols that pervade ritual, whether Christian, Jewish, pagan, Hindu, or archaic. The higher religions have built upon them, and sometimes, especially in the case of Christian rituals, radically reinterpreted them, but they have not abolished them.

Birth, death, and rebirth or resurrection are such a set of images. They occur over and over again in initiatory rituals. Blood is an important ritual image. Its symbolism is always life, not death. The menstrual blood in the girls' initiation ceremonies is an ongoing symbol of their role as life-giver. The antelope blood in the pygmy ritual symbolized the life of the animal. Jews, from Biblical times, will not drink blood, because it is life and life is sacred. Whenever blood is present, the sacred is manifested, and rituals proliferate. Birth rituals and death rituals, for example, usually have to do with blood.

Water is symbolic of both death and rebirth. Waters dissolve and destroy. They also give life. They are formless and give promise of endless possibilities. "Passing through the waters" is always symbolic of death and rebirth. This is true both of individual rites of initiatory washing and of great cosmic myths, such as the flood, the crossing of the River Styx by the souls of the departed, or the passage of the Red Sea by Moses and the Israelites. What went before is dissolved. Entry into the waters marks a temporary return to formlessness, as when the Spirit of God brooded over the waters of chaos at the dawn of creation.[24] To emerge from the waters is to reenact the creation of the cosmos from the waters of chaos. It is the beginning of a new existence. Waters, then, purify, "wash away," and regenerate. This symbolism was known to the Church Fathers and used by them in their explanations of baptism. They dealt quite freely with it, added new meaning and dimension to it, but they did not contradict it. Supernatural meaning was added to natural; grace perfects nature, it does not destroy it.

The Sacred Meal·

Probably the most important symbol is the meal. Certainly it is most significant to us, from our Christian perspective. Alexander Schmemann writes of its significance in the modern world:

> Centuries of secularism have failed to transform eating into something strictly utilitarian. Food is still treated with reverence. A meal is still a rite— the last "natural sacrament" of family and friendship, of life that is more than "eating" and "drinking." To eat is still something more than to maintain bodily functions. People may not understand what that "something more" is, but they nonetheless desire to celebrate it.[25]

Obviously the sacredness of the meal is tied in to all of the primitive ideas we have mentioned concerning hunting, as well as to later but almost as primitive ideas about agriculture. There is, in fact, good reason to believe that the rite we call *sacrifice* is basically a sacred meal. Fr. Louis Bouyer publicized this idea in his book *Rite and Man*:

> What we call by the Latin word "sacrifice" is nothing else than a sacred meal. More specifically, it is every meal that has retained its primitive sacredness, a sacredness that is attached to a meal perhaps more than to any other human action.[26]

Fr. Bouyer appears to have derived his definition from the work of Royden Kieth Yerkes, who wrote:

> The word *sacrifice*, which means "to make a thing sacred" or "to do a sacred act," was used in Latin to describe various rites which arose from the common meal when that meal was held, not for the ordinary purpose of satisfying hunger, but for the purpose of entering into union with the mysterious Power or powers which men felt within them and about them as life itself, and which they recognized in all their environments as both menacing and strengthening the life which they loved and to which they longed to cling.[27]

Dr. Yerkes would look for the origins of sacrifice back to the common meals of the primitive hunters who gathered with their families to eat the meat of their kill.[28] As the killing of a large animal required more than one man, so the eating of the meat would involve more than one family. The sharing of the common meal established a community: the family, the clan, the tribe. Membership in the community entitled one to share in the meal, and the meal itself bound the community together.

Yerkes believes that primitive man sought to share in the qualities of the animals eaten, so that to eat came to mean to share in the life of the victim. Strength, fleetness, wisdom, sexual prowess, could be obtained by eating the flesh of an animal possessing these attributes. The sharing of this power would bind the participants in the meal even closer together.

With the constant repetition of the meal, the tendency of humans (perhaps of all animals) to do the same things in the same way would begin to manifest itself. When people engage in a deliberate group act, they tend to act in repetitive ways, ways we call ritual. The same person leads, the same person cooks, the same person carves. Everyone does the same thing and recites the same words every time the action is performed. This is part of what we mean by corporate action. Otherwise we would have a collection of individual acts, perhaps conflicting with one another.

Yerkes speculates that as human life became more settled the meal came to be held on stated occasions, but was also resorted to in times of crisis, when the need to lay hold on the power to which the meal gave access was acute.

It is widely believed that such a ceremony developed long before the belief in a personal god or gods. Once this belief developed, however, it would be necessary to explain the relationship of the meal to the powers. The meal then came to be seen as a banquet shared by men and divine beings. In some cases it developed into a meal given entirely for the gods, in which the human worshipers did not share.

Where it was believed that the powers to whom the sacrifice was offered lived in the upper air, either in the sky or on a mountaintop, it would be concluded that the portion of the food that passed into the smoke of the cooking fire was that which came in contact with the heavenly powers. In this way, Dr. Yerkes believes, the burning of food on the altar, thereby converting it into smoke, became the prime ingredient of sacrifice in historical times. He even suggests that the Greek word for the gods, the receivers of sacrifice, *theoi*, is derived from the root *thu*, meaning "smoke," from which also the Greek word for sacrifice, *thuein*, is derived.[29]

Whether or not we accept Dr. Yerkes's view of the development of sacrifice, it is clear that the common meal lies behind the classical rites of sacrifice. The practice is certainly much older than any of the explanations given for it. It is a commonplace among students of primitive rituals that the reasons given for performing a rite by those who perform it are seldom the reasons why it was first begun.

We need to beware of assuming that the same practice in different places necessarily has the same meaning. In addition to archetypal symbols that appear to underlie all ritual, and perhaps all of human life, there are many that are culturally conditioned. It seems obvious to us that to remove one's hat is a symbol of respect. This is not true among Jews or Moslems. In America whistling is a form of applause. In Europe its meaning is quite the opposite. Among the ancient Greeks a holocaust, the burning of an entire animal, was a horrible rite of aversion; among the Hebrews the whole burnt offering was the highest form of cultic adoration. We must remember that *cult* and *culture* have a common root.

Fr. Louis Bouyer, in his book *Rite and Man*, examined both the experience of the sacred by primitive man and Jung's analysis of the collective unconscious. He concluded:

> Just as the archetypes of Jung suggest the hierophanies of Eliade, even if they do not reach the point of being completely identifiable with them, so these mythico-ritualistic patterns brought to light by him find remarkable parallels in the models on which, according to Jung, our dreams are built, and in which the ancestral archetypes are awakened to a new life.[30]

If Bouyer is right that we can in some sense identify the images and symbols and mythico-ritual scenarios, such as death and rebirth, which Eliade describes in primitive religions with those which Jung finds in the depths of man's corporate unconscious, then he is undoubtedly right that the primitive rituals relate to something in the foundations of the soul of man, something from which we cannot get away, no matter how civilized and sophisticated we become, as long as we remain human.

NOTES

1. Evelyn Underhill, *Worship* (3rd edition, London: Nisbet, 1937, 1946), p. 3.

2. I was first made aware of this material through reading George Every, *Lamb to the Slaughter* (London: James Clarke, 1957), and I have been strongly influenced by his discussion.

3. Johannes Maringer, *The Gods of Prehistoric Man* (New York: Knopf, 1960), p. 273.

4. *Ibid.*, p. 40.

5. *Ibid.*, p. 272.

6. *Ibid.*, pp. 60-62.

7. Johannes Maringer and Hans-Georg Bandi, *Art in the Ice Age* (New York: Frederick A. Praeger, 1953), p. 10.

8. Maringer, *Gods*, pp. 277f.

9. Adolf E. Jensen, *Myth and Cult among Primitive People* (Chicago: University of Chicago Press, 1963), pp. 253ff.

10. Maringer, *Gods*, p. 148 and Plate IX.

11. *Ibid.*, pp. 150f.

12. Every, *Lamb*, p. 28.

13. Leo Frobenius, *Kulturgeschichte Afrikas* (Zurich, 1933), pp. 127ff; described in Maringer, *Gods*, pp. 130ff.

14. Jensen, *Myth and Cult*, p. 252.

15. Mircea Eliade, *Rites and Symbols of Initiation* (New York: Harper & Row, 1965), p. x.

16. Arnold van Gennep, *The Rites of Passage* (Chicago: University of Chicago Press, 1960), pp. 10f. Van Gennep's book was originally written in 1908 and his terminology has come into general use.

17. Eliade, *Initiation*, p. xv.

18. Maringer, *Gods*, p. 88.

19. *Ibid.*, Ch. II. vi, "Cult of the 'mother goddess.' "

20. The description is synthetic, from the descriptions of actual rites in Eliade, *Initiation*, Ch. I-II, and van Gennep, *Passage*, Ch. VI.

21. Eliade, *Initiation*, pp. 41-47.

22. *Ibid.*, p. 47.

23. *The Hymnal 1940* (New York: Church Hymnal Corp.), Hymn 86.

24. Genesis 1:2.

25. Alexander Schmemann, *For the Life of the World: Sacraments and Orthodoxy* (Crestwood, N.Y.: St. Vladimir's Seminary Press, 1973), p. 16.

26. Louis Bouyer, *Rite and Man* (Notre Dame: University of Notre Dame Press, 1963), p. 82.

27. Royden K. Yerkes, *Sacrifice in Greek and Roman Religious and Early Judaism* (London: Adam and Charles Black, 1953), pp. 25f.

28. *Ibid.*, Ch. III, "Early Development of Sacrifice."

29. *Ibid.*, p. 24.

30. Bouyer, *Rite*, p. 51.

2
Background of Christian Worship

In the preceding chapter we spoke of the beginning of ritual worship and of the place of ritual in the life of primitive man. We emphasized particularly the rites of sacrifice and initiation and the common symbols underlying most ritual. We now turn to a discussion of the religious rituals that would actually have been familiar to the earliest Christians.

Christian and Pagan Rituals

At least from the time of Justin Martyr in the second century, Christians have been aware of certain parallels between their rites and those of the Hellenistic mystery religions. Justin had a simple explanation for the parallels. They were introduced by the devil to confound the faithful.[1] When the same parallels were pointed out in a more scientific manner in the first decades of this century by the practitioners of the new discipline of the history of religions, they felt that they had reduced Christianity to one of a number of basically similar Near Eastern mystery cults which acted out in a ritual the death and return to life of a savior god.[2] Christians naturally responded by attempting to assert

23

the uniqueness and divine origin of the Christian sacraments. The stage seemed set for another conflict between "religion" and "science."

The most creative response to this challenge was that of Dom Odo Casel, monk of Maria Laach, whose work has been called by Joseph Jungmann "one of the most important Catholic contributions to the study of comparative religion and the history of primitive Christianity."[3] Casel made no attempt to deny the contentions of his opponents that Christian rites were organically related to pagan ones. Instead he argued from the truth of Christianity that the rites of the pagan mysteries were a divinely provided preparation for the Christian gospel and sacraments, which made it possible for converts to understand the meaning of the rites they experienced.[4]

Contemporary scholars would not be as willing as Casel was to accept the factual claims of the "history of religions school." They see many borrowings from Christianity by the pagan cults, as well as significant Jewish sources for the external forms of Christian worship. Most scholars today would retreat from Casel's admission that "Christianity is of its own very essence . . . a mystery religion,"[5] but many of his basic ideas have been incorporated into the best contemporary liturgical theology, and they found expression in the Constitution on the Sacred Liturgy of Vatican Council II.[6]

Casel's vision is of Christianity as the fulfillment of natural religion. He saw in the Christian sacraments that toward which the rites of other religions were groping, the reality of which other rites were types and shadows. He saw clearly that to show that the Christian Eucharist, for example, is related to primitive meal-sacrifices does not imply that the Eucharist is not unique, nor divinely instituted. It tends rather to show that God has led men throughout history to seek him in a sacred meal, and that a study of sacred meals will provide us with one level of knowledge about the Eucharist, i.e. that it is a common meal binding together those who share it. On the other hand, we must remember that its differences from other sacred meals are at least as important as its similarities. Those differences are at the level not of ritual form but of inner meaning.

The study of comparative religions leads some people to conclude that all religions are equally true, that it matters not at all whether I am a Baptist or a Buddhist, an Episcopalian, Roman Catholic, Moslem, or Hindu, for all are specific cultural developments of natural religions. The same line of thought leads others to conclude that all religions are equally false, either primitive superstitions or priestly confidence games of which modern man has no need. It is against these extreme views that, following Casel, I would say that ritual worship indeed first appeared among primitive men, for it corresponds to something central to human nature. We do not outgrow it, but it develops in complexity and sophistication along with us. This development accounts for the similarities among the rituals of mankind, but it is only in Christianity that the rituals are fulfilled. The incarnation of the Son of God and his mighty acts in the redemption of the human race provide the content of Christian rituals, a content that was able to fill the ritual forms earlier religion had provided.

Historically Christian rituals depend upon Jewish rituals, and to a lesser extent upon other religious ritu-

als of the Hellenistic era. A great deal of work has been
done in this century to demonstrate the Jewish origins
of Christian rites,[7] and the basic point may be taken as
proven. The Jewish rites themselves, however, are a
reinterpretation and historicization of more general ritual forms.

Christian rites, then, did not appear fully developed upon the scene. They represent a new *valorization*,
or building upon, rites that already existed in the first
century A.D. They were infused with new meanings that
completely transformed their inner nature, but they
have the rites and symbols of natural religion and the
specific reinterpretation of those rites by Judaism as
their necessary foundation.

Sacrifice in the Ancient World

Let us look, then, at the concept of *sacrifice* as it
was known to the Greek and Jewish religions of the
time of Christ. Unfortunately the meaning of the word
sacrifice in contemporary English is so colored by the
theological controversies of the Reformation period,
and by its secular use, as to make it difficult for us to
understand its ancient meaning.

We have already seen that the word was used to
describe various rites that derive from the common
meal. Dr. Yerkes lists six ways in which the ancient
idea of sacrifice differs substantially from ours:

1. Sacrifice in the ancient world had no secular
meaning whatever. Unlike other words that were bor-
rowed from secular usage for religious purposes, such
as liturgy or eucharist, sacrifice had no meaning except
to celebrate a sacred rite.

2. Sacrifices were occasions of joy and festivity.

The word never connoted the acceptance of unavoidable loss or deprivation. They were feasts that joyfully expressed the relationship of men to their gods.

3. Because they were occasions of joy and festivity, sacrifices were always as large as possible. There was no idea of getting as good a bargain as possible, since the sacrifice was gladly and freely given.

4. Sacrifices were offered *by* men *to* their gods. The emphasis was on the *giving*, not the giving *up*. It is unquestionably true that if you give something away you no longer have it, but the giver's concern is with the recipient, not his own loss of the gift. The idea of a sacrifice not offered *to* someone would have been incomprehensible.

5. Sacrifices were frequently offered as expressions of thanksgiving for a boon already received. It was not unknown to offer sacrifice as a petition for some divine favor, but it was at least as common to offer a sacrifice of thanksgiving. There is little of the idea of a "business deal" in which the worshiper gives "so much" and the god gives "so much."

6. (This is the most important point.) The death of the animal, while a necessary fact preliminary to the sacrifice, was never a *factor* in the sacrifice. When an animal was sacrificed it had to be killed, but the killing was not the sacrifice. It was always done with restraint and ceremony, "but no significance was ever attached to the fact that the animal had died. We never hear of death *qua* death effecting anything."[8]

Dr. Yerkes believes, as does Fr. Bouyer, that the confounding of *death* and sacrifice is the starting point for most of the difficulties we have experienced in understanding sacrifice. The central core of the sacrifice is the sharing of the common meal by worshiper and god. If the meal includes meat, that requires the death of an animal, as it still does. We do not normally consider the slaughter of a steer to be a part of our Sunday barbecue, but unquestionably there would be no roast beef without it. There were sacrifices of grain and wine in the ancient world, and they, of course, did not involve slaughter.

Dr. Yerkes has, perhaps, overstated the case slightly, since the ritual slaughter of the victim was clearly a part of the rite, but he is certainly right that we shall never understand the significance of sacrifice in the New Testament if we focus on the death of the victim. Certainly the modern secular idea of a sacrifice as something we give up in order to obtain a greater reward, as in baseball, chess, and business, can only confuse our understanding.

Finally, we should notice that the most common association of sacrifice was with thanksgiving. The idea of sacrifice as a propitiation for sin is late medieval and is found neither in Scripture nor in natural religion.[9] What are called "sin-offerings" in the English translations of the Old Testament are actually not sacrifices properly so-called; they are purificatory rites intended to remove ritual uncleanness so that a person may participate in the offering of a sacrifice. When moral perfection came to be seen as part of what God required of man, then the "uncleanness" might be moral as well as simply the violation of a ritual taboo, but the sacrifice proper was not the "sin-offering." It was the feast to which the removal of the impurity readmitted the worshipper.

Sacrifice in Judaism

With these warnings in mind, we can say that the rituals of Christian worship developed over centuries and millennia into forms suitable for fulfilling the divine purpose. Jesus chose to institute the distinctive rite of his New Covenant at a sacred meal, and to use elements already filled with symbolic meaning: bread and wine. He gave new meanings to an already highly developed ritual form, the common meal, and specifically to that meal in its Jewish religious form.

In Judaism the sacrifice developed in three distinct ways. (1) Formal cultic sacrifices were offered in the Jerusalem Temple. (2) A distinctive form of ritual slaughter known as kosher butchering arose. (3) The religious meal became an important element in Jewish life.

Like the Ice Age hunters at whom we looked in the last chapter, the ancient Jews believed that all life was sacred, and refused to kill anything outsude of a ritual context. To take the things of God for ourselves without permission is sacrilege. God is therefore involved in every stage of the preparation of food.

The Pesach

The oldest Hebrew sacrifice is the *pesach* (Passover). It is specifically of interest to us as Christians since it was at the Passover that Jesus was crucified, and the Last Supper is itself identified with the Passover meal in the synoptic gospels.[10] It was so central to St. Paul's understanding that he could say, "Christ our *pesach* has been sacrificed, therefore let us celebrate the festival."[11] It seems, therefore, an appropriate place to begin.

The *pesach* is one of the oldest religious festivals still celebrated in the world. It has been kept for at least twenty-five hundred years, but is probably much older than our oldest records. It is celebrated in the night of the first full moon of spring, which for the ancient Hebrews was the first full moon of the year. In its original form it was celebrated at home, with the head of the household officiating. It required the intervention of neither priest nor temple. Its central action was the sacrifice of a spring lamb to Yahweh.[12]

We do not know the actual origin of the sacrifice. It has been offered to Yahweh for at least twenty-five centuries. In a prehistoric stage the lamb was probably identified with the divine power man wanted to understand and to appropriate to himself. To eat the *pesach* was to learn one's own complete dependence on God.

Later a new meaning was added. The *pesach* commemorated the exodus from Egypt. The account in the Book of Exodus hints that the feast is really older than Moses, since it was to keep a feast to Yahweh in the wilderness that Moses asks Pharaoh to let the people go.[13] The historical commemoration of the exodus, however, became the principal meaning of the festival. To the present day the master of the *seder* proclaims at the celebration:

We were Pharaoh's salves in Egypt, and the Lord our God brought us forth from there with a mighty hand and an outstretched arm. And if the Holy One, blessed be he, had not brought our forefathers forth from Egypt, then we, our children, and our children's children would still be Pharaoh's slaves in Egypt.

So, even though all of us were wise, all of us full of understanding, all of us elders, all of us knowing in the Torah, we should still be under the commandment to tell the story of the departure from Egypt.

And the more one tells the story of the departure from Egypt, the more praiseworthy he is.[14]

The purpose of the *pesach* has become the remembrance of God's mighty act in the exodus, to which Israel owes its existence as a people, and which manifests Israel's total dependence upon its God. But it is not simply an historical commemoration. It is a ritual renewal of the event of the exodus. The participants in the celebration are themselves redeemed:

> In every generation let each man look on himself as if he came forth from Egypt.
> As it is said: "And thou shalt tell thy son in that day, saying: It is because of that which the Lord did for me when I came forth out of Egypt."

> It was not only our fathers that the Holy One, blessed be he, redeemed, but us as well did he redeem along with them.
> And it is said: "And he brought us out from thence, that He might bring us in, to give us the land which He swore unto our fathers."

> Therefore, we are bound to thank, praise, laud, glorify, exalt, honor, bless, extol, and adore Him who performed all these miracles for our fathers and for us. He has brought us forth from slavery to freedom, from sorrow to joy, from mourning to holiday, from darkness to great light, and from bondage to redemption.[15]

The Passover, as it is still celebrated by Jews, is a festival of the freedom of God's people, giving thanks to God for his continued sustenance. Christians, of course, have added another layer of meaning, since it was at the Passover that Jesus was crucified and rose again, and it was in the context of the Passover meal that Jesus instituted the Eucharist with his disciples. And so the traditional Easter liturgy proclaims:

> This is the night, when you brought our fathers, the children of Israel, out of bondage in Egypt, and let them through the Red Sea on dry land. This is the night, when all who believe in Christ are delivered from the gloom of sin and are restored to grace and holiness of life. This is the night, when Christ broke the bonds of death and hell, and rose victorious from the grave.[16]

We echo the words of St. Paul that Christ is the true *pesach* whose blood delivers his people from slavery to sin and death.

The essence of the *pesach* is the eating of a roast lamb which has been offered to Yahweh.[17] It is eaten in haste, totally consumed. Nothing is to remain until the morning. Leftovers are to be burned. This strongly suggests the feast of a band of Nomads: a celebration "on the run" with great care taken not to leave a trail for their enemies to follow. A "blood rite" forms an integral part of the celebration. The door is marked with the blood of the lamb, to purify the house in which the sacrifice will be eaten.

It is worth noting that no particular significance was attached to the fact that the lamb was killed; the "blood rite" and the feast upon the flesh were the significant ritual acts. It is also worth noting that no portion of the lamb was reserved for Yahweh. It was to be completely eaten by the worshipers who in that way showed their trust in Yahweh and their total dependence upon Him.

The "blood rite" is explained in Exodus 12:23 by reference to the exodus. It is the mark that protects the homes of the Israelites from the angel of death. Since the mark made with the blood was an "X," Christians further reinterpreted the "blood rite" to signify the redemption of the world by the blood of Christ, the lamb slain from the foundation of the world, identifying the "X" mark either with the Greek *chi*, the first letter of "Christos," or with the sign of the cross. There is little doubt, however, that the Jewish explanation, as much as the Christian, is a later addition to explain an ancient rite of which the original meaning had been forgotten.

In the days when the Hebrews were nomadic shepherd people they celebrated a spring lamb sacrifice, the *pesach*. They marked their doors with the blood and feasted on the flesh. Probably, the blood was to ward off evil so that the family could gather behind the door to eat the lamb. The roast lamb was eaten by families, with the father presiding. Its original meaning probably was related to the spring lambing season. It came to be seen as a recognition of total dependence on Yahweh, who makes the lambs to bring forth young, and thereby clothes and feeds his people. To this is added the commemoration of the exodus, which completely overshadows the earlier meanings, and then Christians have reinterpreted its meaning in terms of Christ as the *pesach*.

The Feast of Unleavened Bread

From at least the time of the writing of the Biblical accounts, the *pesach* has been combined with an agricultural feast, *matzoth*, the Feast of Unleavened Bread, so that the two came to be considered a single feast. The *pesach*, the lamb sacrifice, however, is clearly older, since the unleavened bread is the festival of a settled agricultural society. It is an agricultural festival of annual renewal that probably originated with the nature worship of the Canaanites. Its root meaning is the offering of the first fruits of the barley harvest, baked into fresh bread.[18] Since it was a new crop, no part of the old was mixed with it. The new grain was offered to the Lord of the harvest in thanksgiving for the gift of food.

The normal method of making bread rise was to keep the dough and allow it to ferment. A small portion of this "leaven" mixed in the dough would make the bread rise. When the new loaves were baked each year from the first fruits of the new crop, there would be no "leaven" since last year's dough would not be mixed with the new. The Feast of Unleavened Bread lasted eight days. By then there would be new "leaven" to make the bread rise. The new bread, like the new lamb, marked a renewal of the year, a beginning.

The Feast of Unleavened Bread was itself given an historical interpretation in Exodus 12:39 as part of its identification with *pesach*. It was, therefore, the combined festival that was celebrated in the time of Christ, and the idea of the renewal of growing things became a part of the background of the Christian Easter.

The Passover Ritual Today

Today the Jewish celebration of the Passover has become quite ceremonious. It includes a great deal of instruction intended to explain to the children the meaning of the rituals and to play an important part in their integration into the Jewish community. Every special food that is eaten is explained, but obviously the ceremonies are themselves older than the explanation. Ironically, the *pesach*, the lamb, is no longer eaten by the Jews. As part of the Deuteronomic reforms, the sacrifice of the lamb, like all other sacrifice, was restricted to the Jerusalem Temple,[19] and since the destruction of the Temple in 70 A.D. Jews have substituted for the lamb a shank-bone.

The meal ritual itself is called *seder*, which means *order*; that is, the order in which the ceremonies are performed. The text of the prayers and the directions concerning the performance of the ceremonies are called the *Haggadah*, and are today printed as a book for use at the *seder*. Many of the customs of the meal are simply those traditional at dinner in the ancient world, but others have religious meaning.

Many descriptions of the meaning of the *seder* as celebrated by Jews today are available, and this description will confine itself to the most important ritual acts that probably were a part of the rite at the time of Christ.

The meal begins with the *kiddush*, a blessing over a cup of wine. There are really two blessings said, one giving thanks for the wine, and one thanking God for the festival being celebrated.

The ritual washing of hands is done by Jews at the beginning of all solemn religious meals. This is partially a practical necessity, but is also a symbol of the purity with which we approach God.

The special ceremonies of the *pesach* follow. A second cup of wine is poured and the narrative of the exodus is read. The special foods: the lamb (today represented by a shank-bone), bitter herbs, and unleavened bread, are explained.

The bread is then blessed and broken, as it is at the beginning of all Jewish meals, and the meal begins.

After the meal a third cup of wine is poured and over it is said a long prayer of blessing, giving thanks to God for the food, the land, and the people of Israel. This too is a common feature of Jewish religious meals.

Finally the Hallelujah psalms, called the *hallel*, are sung and a fourth cup of wine is drunk.

We shall come back to this description when we talk about the origin of the Christian Eucharist. What we have in this meal, in its earlier form, is the most important of the Jewish sacrifices. It differed from the other sacrifices in that it was totally eaten by the worshipers, and in that it did not originally involve the priests or the temple.

Sacrifices in the Temple

The Old Testament provides us with a great deal of detailed information about the formal sacrifices of the Jerusalem Temple. Without following their various forms and varieties, it is possible to say some general things about their ritual pattern. This ritual pattern that we find in the Hebrew *zebach* is substantially the same as that of the Greek *thusia*.[20] It would therefore correspond in a rough way to the common understanding of *sacrifice* in Hellenistic culture.

The sacrifice may be thought of as having three stages:

1. The first is *the preparation*. The worshipers must be themselves ritually clean. This was not neces-

sarily originally a moral state, although it came in Judaism to include moral purity. If the worshiper was "unclean" because he had violated some ritual taboo, an appropriate rite of purification would have to precede the sacrifice. They would then prepare the victim, by choosing it for the sacrifice. It was necessary that the victim belong to the worshiper and that it be a perfect animal. Sick or deformed animals were not proper subjects for sacrifice.

The animal was then brought to the place of sacrifice and offered to Yahweh. The worshiper laid his hand upon the sacrifice, apparently to identify it as his own offering, and then he killed it. The third chapter of Leviticus anticipates that the worshiper will kill the animal himself. It was only after the animal had been slain that the priest began his part. The priests took the blood of the slain victim and used it to purify the altar.

An important feature of this preparation section in the Greek *thusia* was the *euche*, the prayer setting forth the purpose of the sacrifice and accompanied by the scattering of grains of barley.

2. *The sacrifice proper* consisted of the burning of certain parts of the animal upon the altar. This obviously required that the animal be butchered, which would have been the most time-consuming part of the rite.

3. The concluding act was *the feast* upon the flesh of the animal. The Greeks roasted the flesh for the banquet, while the Jews boiled it, but in both cases the joyful feast shared by priests and people formed the conclusion of the rite. It was in a real sense a communion feast shared by mortals and God, and it was this feast that was the most obvious feature of sacrifice in the ancient world.

In the Jewish rites the blood, which is the symbol

of the life, is returned to its source; appropriate parts of the animal are returned to the deity; and man is free to eat the meat. One purpose of the sacrifice was to remove the taboo against killing, to avoid blood-guilt by offering the life back to God in accordance with the divinely given directions.

In Judaism a form of the sacrifice developed, the *'olah*, in which all of the meat was burnt upon the altar, and this was considered to be the highest and most joyful form of sacrifice.[21] This is a later development and became prominent only after the exile. It was an act of thanksgiving and worship of Yahweh. Originally it was believed that the aroma of the burning animal was pleasing to him. The development of the *'olah* is apparently related to the development of Deuteronomic sacrificial theology that considered the sacrifice a *qorban*, a gift to God. Once this principle became established, the giving of the complete animal to the Lord, keeping none for oneself, came easily to symbolize complete surrender to Yahweh, and the total joy of giving onself to the Lord.

The *zebach*, in which only a portion of the food was offered to the Lord, emphasized communion with God. The *pesach*, in which the worshipers ate all of the food, emphasized total dependence on God. The *'olah* symbolized total devotion to God.

Obviously none of these sacrifical forms carried over into Christianity. Christians do not offer animal sacrifices, nor do modern Jews. But the inner meaning of these sacrifical rites has remained central to Jewish and Christian religious life: complete devotion to God, total dependence upon Him and the desire to live as He wills, and joyful cooperation and communion with the Creator in His work.

Rites of Purification

We have already mentioned the various rites of purification, the so-called "sin offerings" which are associated with sacrifices in the Old Testament. It was not the purpose of the sacrifices we have been considering to remove sin. One who had committed sin could not offer them. The Old Testament also contains rites of purification, both from ritual faults and from moral ones. The most impressive of these are the rites of Yom Kippur, the Day of Atonement, which are given a Christian interpretation in the Epistle to the Hebrews. The rites themselves are ancient and complex.[22] Their purpose is to purify the priests, the sanctuary, and the whole people of Israel so that they may be able to celebrate the Feast of Tabernacles. The purification was accomplished with blood, the most powerful purifying agent they knew, but the animal whose blood was used to purify the priests and the holy of holies was not offered to the Lord. It was neither burned on the altar nor eaten by anyone. It was hauled away "outside the camp" and burned. This, incidentally, is the point of Hebrews 13:10-16, distinguishing the sacrifice of Christ, which was offered to God on the heavenly altar itself and of which we have been commanded to eat in the Eucharist, from the Jewish "sin offerings" which were burned ouside the camp.

Kosher Butchering

The second stream of Jewish sacrificial rites is not of particular concern to us. Kosher butchering is a development of the Deuteronomic restriction of sacrifice to the Jerusalem Temple. It is a rite for the ritual slaughter of animals for meat. The animal is killed to the accompaniment of prayer, and the blood is poured out to the Lord, thereby freeing the meat for human consumption. The Orthodox Jew will eat only meat from animals killed in this way.

The Jewish Religious Meal

The third stream is the Jewish religious meal. The *seder* at Passover is, of course, the Jewish religious meal par excellence, and in it the relationship of the meal to sacrifice is most clear. But on every sabbath and on every feast a religious meal is eaten by observant Jews to this day. It was at such a meal that Jesus instituted the Eucharist.

The typical sacred meal of Judaism is the Friday night dinner which inaugurates the celebration of the sabbath. It is still observed in Jewish homes and is one of the marks of Jewish religious observance. We know that in the time of Christ similar formal religious meals were held by rabbis and their disciples.

We are not actually sure whether the meal Jesus ate with his disciples at the Last Supper was the Passover meal, or an ordinary religious meal. The Scriptural accounts differ. The synoptic gospels say it was the Passover, while St. John says that the Passover began at sundown the following day, Good Friday, so that the Passover that year coincided with the sabbath. According to St. John's Gospel, Jesus died precisely at the time when the lambs were being slain for the *pesach*. In both cases the desire is to identify Jesus with the true *pesach*. It is clear that he died at Passover, and the spirit of that festival pervaded all that happened in the minds of the evangelists.

Whether the Last Supper was the Passover meal or not, Jesus made no use of the specific paschal ceremonies we described above. The blessing of the bread and wine are parts of the common structure the *seder* shares with other meals.

The sabbath meal, the typical Jewish sacred meal, begins with the lighting of the candles. They are lighted by the mother before sundown, the actual beginning of the sabbath. The lighting is accompanied by prayer.

When all are seated a cup of wine is poured and the *kiddush* is recited. This is a blessing of the festival day that is now beginning. It is said at the beginning of the sabbath and other festivals. This is the form in which it is recited at Passover:

Blessed art thou, O Lord our God, king of the universe, who chose us from every people, and exalted us among every tongue, and sanctified us by his commandments. With love thou hast given us, O Lord our God, holidays for gladness, [Sabbaths for rest] festivals and seasons for rejoicing, this [Sabbath day and this] day of the festival of unleavened bread, the season of our deliverance, [with love] a holy convocation in remembrance of the departure from Egypt. For thou hast chosen us, and us hast thou sanctified from all peoples. [And the Sabbath] and the holidays of thy sanctification [with love and favor] hast thou given us, with gladness and joy to inherit. Blessed are thou, O Lord, who sanctifies [the Sabbath and] Israel and the seasons.[23]

A different form is used on ordinary sabbaths and on other festivals. We cannot be certain how old these prayers are, but the Mishna, in the second century A.D., describes a controversy in the Rabbinic schools over whether it was proper to say the blessing of the day or the blessing of the wine first.[24] This would indicate that some form of these blessings was already ancient at that time. Today the blessing of the day is preceded by a blessing of the cup of wine, but since that was precisely the matter under dispute by the rabbis, we do not know whether it preceded or followed in the first century. The text is quite simple:

> Blessed art thou, O Lord our God, King of the universe who createst the fruit of the vine.[25]

It is possible that the Gospel according to St. Luke (22:17-18) has this initial cup of wine before the meal in mind when it says:

> And he took a cup and when he had given thanks he said, "Take this, and divide it among yourselves; for I tell you that I shall not drink of the fruit of the vine until the kingdom of God comes."

The *kiddush* is immediately followed by the blessing of bread, which is the formal beginning of every meal:

> Blessed art thou, O Lord our God, King of the universe, who bringest forth bread from the earth.[26]

The father holds the bread in his hand while he says the blessing, and then breaks and distributes it to those who are at the table, eating a piece himself. There can be no reasonable doubt that it was at this point in the ritual of the Last Supper that Jesus said, "This is my body." The ceremonial described in the gospel is identical with that of the Jewish ritual, and we may assume that "when he had given thanks" refers to His recitation of the proper blessing over the bread.

The blessing used at the Passover is the same as that used upon all other occasions. It is recited over the *matzoth*, the unleavened bread, but the same words are used.

The breaking of the bread with the recitation of the blessing marked the formal beginning of the meal. The meal itself was a religious event, the fellowship and conversation as well as the prayers. Dr. Frank Gavin, a distinguished Christian student of Jewish rites, described it this way:

> It was entirely in accord with the spirit of Judaism so to hallow social intercourse, or, to put it the other way about, to deem social intercourse sacred. The common meal, with its accompaniment of conversation on matters of the Law, the administration of charity, or the religious and spiritual interests of the company, would so closely approximate what we should name "sacred" as to suggest an unjustified contrast to "secular." But we have seen that this antithesis, this dichotomy of life, was alien and repugnant to Judaism. Sacred and profane, religious and secular, devotional and worldly, were never construed as opposites or contrasts.[27]

Certainly it must have been such a group as Dr. Gavin describes that met in the Upper Room with the Rabbi Jesus for the Last Supper. Certainly, too, they must have met similarly for many suppers before. The sharing of food by a master and his disciples, or by a natural family keeping the sabbath or a festival, is already a sacred act.

The chief prayer in the ritual comes at the close of the meal. It is recited over a cup of wine. This is the "cup of blessing" mentioned by St. Paul.[28] It is introduced by a dialogue that is mentioned in the Mishna.[29] Our earliest surviving text of the prayer itself is from the eighth century,[30] but the distinguished Jewish scholar Louis Finklestein has proposed this reconstruction of the first century text:

We will bless him of whose bounty we have partaken. *Blessed be he of whose bounty we have partaken, and through whose goodness we live.*

Blessed art thou, O Lord our God, King of the universe, who feedest the whole world in goodness, kindness, and mercy. Blessed art thou, O Lord, who feedest all.

We give thee thanks, O Lord our God, who hast given us this good land for our heritage that we may eat of its fruits and be satisfied with its goodness. Blessed art thou, O Lord our God, for the land and for the food.

Have mercy, O Lord our God, upon Israel thy people and Jerusalem thy city and Sion the dwelling-place of thy glory and of thy altar, and of thy sanctuary. Blessed art thou, O Lord, who buildest Jerusalem.[31]

In the tradition represented by I Corinthians 11:25 and St. Luke 22:20 which speak of "the cup after supper," it was at this point in the Last Supper that our Lord spoke the words over the cup:

> And he took a cup, and when he had given thanks he gave it to them and they all drank of it. And he said to them, "This is my blood of the covenant, which is poured out for many."[32]

Both St. Mark (quoted here) and St. Matthew refer to the giving of thanks over the cup, which sounds like a reference to the traditional Jewish prayer, while St. Luke and I Corinthians use the adverb "likewise" to refer to their mention of giving thanks over the bread. There does not seem to be any real doubt that this "cup of blessing" is the source of the eucharistic chalice, and the prayer of thanksgiving said over it the source of the Christian eucharistic prayer.

During the prayer the father holds the cup of wine in both hands and lifts it. At its close all drink.

These actions at the beginning and ending of the meal were common to all formal meals eaten by observant Jews. The special ritual of the Passover incorporated these actions into a more complex rite, but it was the common blessing of bread before the meal and the prayer said over the cup of wine at its conclusion that were given new meaning by Jesus in his institution of the rite of the New Covenant. In this way we find the ancient common meal coming into Christianity through Judaism. It carries with it a great freight of ancient meanings, the idea of thanksgiving to God for food, and life, and fellowship, and the act of communion, or fellowship, with those with whom we eat. St. Paul sees a clear parallel between Christian participation in the Lord's Supper and participation in the Greek sacrificial feasts, as he writes to the Corinthians:

> What pagans sacrifice they offer to demons and not to God. I do not want you to be partners with demons. You cannot drink the cup of the Lord and the cup of demons. You cannot partake of the table of the Lord and the table of demons.[33]

The common religious meal is a meeting, not only of individuals who share in a social act, but also of God and man. St. Paul is concerned that what we would call ordinary social activity not involve the Christians of Corinth in the worship of the pagan gods, even indirectly.

Classical Pagan Rites

We need to remember that classical paganism, the worship of the Olympian gods, was by no means dead in the first century. The public sacrifices to the patron deities of the various cities were solemnly offered by the appropriate priests and magistrates. They were well attended and seen to be necessary to the well-being of the state. We might almost say that the official religion was too public. Its significance was in the area of the relationship of Zeus or Athena to the city and its needs. It said little about the religious needs of individuals. It had, perhaps, become what we call today a "civil religion." This does not mean that it was not faithfully, even fanatically practiced. The unwillingness of Christians to participate in these ceremonies probably called forth the same range of emotions we have seen in our own time when protesters against the Vietnam War burned the American flag, or when black athletes at the 1972 Olympics refused to stand at attention during the Star Spangled Banner. Classical paganism in the first century A.D. may no longer have been the religion of the Homeric epics, but it was far from dead.

We have already seen that the *thusia*, the classical Greek sacrifice, was quite similar to the Hebrew *zebach* in general structure and meaning. The Romanization of the Greek gods and their identification with Latin deities is too well known to require further comment. Greek rituals also, not surprisingly, exerted great influence on Roman practice, but they were always considered to be foreign. The native Roman rituals were quite different from those we have examined. The purpose of all Roman rites was propitiation, i.e., retaining the favor of friendly supernatural powers and driving away hostile ones.[34] They did not develop the joyous sacrificial meal shared by men and gods. In typical Roman rites the victim was carefully prepared and slaughtered, the *exta* (the vital organs) were examined, and if they were free from defect burned upon the altar. Any form of defect rendered the victim unfit for sacrificial use. The rites were conducted in absolute silence. Dr. Yerkes comments:

> The important feature of Roman religious rites was the precision of ceremonial prescribed and required by the *ius divinum*, which carefully protected and regulated all rites. To make a single mistake in word or act would necessitate repeating the whole rite from the beginning. . . . The lugubrious precision and silence with which they were conducted preserved their quasi-magical character

and gave a peculiar turn to the development of Roman religious ideas.[35]

Inevitably the same idea of ritual worship came to affect Christianity when it was imported to Rome. The Roman idea of sacrifice was so different from that of the Greeks and the Jews that the mere translation of the term "sacrifice of thanksgiving" from Greek into Latin would give a different tone to the discussion. Certainly the intrusion of Roman ideas of the meaning of sacrifice upon the Christian use of the term must bear a share in the confusion and conflict that have surrounded discussion of the sacrificial nature of the Eucharist.

The Mystery Cults

The great personal religious rituals of the Hellenistic world and the real competitors of Christianity were the mystery religions. Unfortunately we do not know a great deal about them, since their rites were secret, and severe penalties were attached to divulging them. They were built upon the primitive themes of initiation. They were secret societies that revealed to their initiates the way of salvation, although it is not always clear exactly what that salvation was. They were nonexclusive, and it was not unusual for devotees to be initiated into several mysteries. Even the great philosophers were initiated into the mysteries. Plato, for example, wrote in the *Phaedo*:

I fancy that those men who established the mysteries were not unenlightened, but in reality had a hidden meaning when they said long ago that whoever goes uninitiated and unsanctified to the other world will lie in the mire, but he who arrives there initiated and purified will dwell with the gods. For as they say in the mysteries, "the thyrsus-bearers are many, but the mystics few"; and these mystics are, I believe, those who have been true philosophers. And I in my life have, so far as I could, left nothing undone and have striven in every way to make myself one of them.[36]

In the *Phaedrus* he gives an even more glowing description of initiation into the mysteries:

At that former time they saw beauty shining in brightness, when, with a blessed company—we following in the train of Zeus, and others in that of some other god—they saw the blessed sight and vision and were initiated into that which is rightly called the most blessed of mysteries, which we celebrated in a state of perfection, when we were without experience of the evils which awaited us in the time to come, being permitted as initiates to the sight of perfect and simple and calm apparitions, which we saw in a pure light, being ourselves pure and not entombed in this which we carry about with us and call the body, in which we are imprisoned like an oyster in its shell.[37]

But the explanations, even of a Plato, were extrinsic to the mysteries, which were rites, pure and simple, into which the *mystai* were initiated. It was the performance of the rite itself that was believed to give salvation. Odo Casel gives this useful definition of a mystery rite:

The mystery is a sacred ritual action in which a saving deed is made present through the rite; the congregation, by performing the rite, take part in the saving act, and thereby win salvation.[38]

The content of the mysteries was the repetition, the making present, of the mythic events of a first age. They reveal a vision of the world of true reality, the meaning of which can be grasped only through the rite:

The saving, healing act of God is performed over and over. Worship is the means of making it real once more, and thus of breaking through to the spring of salvation. The members of the cult present again in a ritual, symbolic fashion, that primeval act; in holy words and rites of priest and faithful the reality is there once more. The celebrant community is united in the deepest fashion with the Lord they worship; there is no deeper oneness than suffering and action shared. Thereby they win a share in the new life of God; they enter his chorus, they become gods. The mysteries' way is, therefore, the way of ritual action as a sharing in the gods' acts; its aim is union with godhead, share in his life.[39]

The *kyrios*, the lord of the mystery, is a divine being who has suffered, died, and was restored to life, and is thereby the means of conquering death for his devotees. This is what Casel considers the great contribution of the mystery religions to the understanding of Christianity:

The mystery is the buried god; that Jahwe, the God of the Old Testament could lie in a grave is unthinkable. For the Greeks as well who thought of their gods on Olympus radiant with beauty and power, health and freshness, a god in a grave was equally inconceivable. But the mystery religions do know such a god, who bears the deepest fate of man, even death; who bears it to the end and so overcomes it and gives the initiate the hope that he too may overcome and win a share in the everlasting life of god. "Take courage, *mystai*, for the god is saved; for us too sorrow shall be turned to saving." Here is a mysterious foreshadowing of what Christianity has brought; for we too give honor to a buried god.[40]

We have already mentioned the complex question of the relationship of these rites to Christianity. Modern scholarship has put to rest the contention of the "history of religions school" that Christian sacramental rites are actually derived from those of the mysteries.[41] Certainly, though, there is a real relationship. The mystery religions unquestionably provided a background against which Gentile converts to Christianity could view the Christian rites. A mystery cult origin has been suggested for many statements of the early Church. On the other hand, it has been appropriately pointed out that St. Paul does not hesitate to correct the mystery-theology of Hellenistic converts. In Romans 6, for example, he makes clear that we have not already been raised from death with Christ, but that this is an eschatological hope: "But if we have died with Christ, we believe that we also *shall live* (future) with him."[42]

The Hellenistic mystery religions were rituals. There was no "religion" beyond the performance of the rite. It was the participation in the rite itself that gave salvation. But the Christian "mystery" is not a rite; it is the revelation of the mighty acts of God himself in Christ. Christians have never taught that mere participation in the rites of the Church, without any inward conversion of life, will win salvation. Christianity did not hesitate to adopt the terms of the mystery cults, and to alter and adapt them to make clear to converts from paganism the meaning of the salvation the gospel proclaimed; but they did not derive either their rites or their basic theology from them.

One way to express this would be to say that there is in human nature something that makes ritual work, something that makes us express symbolically what is deep within us. It is part of our nature to act out, to symbolize, what we perceive as spiritual truth. If, as Genesis declares, God made us in his image, then we should not be surprised that when he wished to communicate spiritual truth to us he acted in a symbolic, ritual way. He became man, and he used rituals to express his meaning.

The origin of the mystery cults lies in agricultural rites and the meaning of the seed that is sown in the earth and grows again. It has been suggested that these agricultural rites themselves derive from the rites of women's initiation. One contemporary writer expresses it this way:

The mysteries of Demeter at Eleusis, the cult of the Egyptian Isis, the worship of the Great Mother in Asia Minor, are such initiations associated with agriculture, gradually drawing in, not only the peasantry, but citizens and rulers fascinated by mystery, until in their latter days they became means of grace, whereby men rather than women, but not men alone, were initiated into something deeper than gardening, corn-growing or child-bearing, into some renewal of generation that would not decay or decline with the death of nations, but might provide a passport to re-establishment not here in the next generation, but in happier fields in another world.[43]

The Greek mysteries, such as the Eleusinian mysteries, which numbered among their initiates most of the important figures of the classical world, passed through three or four distinct stages of development.[44]

In the first stage the mysteries are simply the agricultural rites of a farming community, celebrating the growth of the apparently dead and buried seed, and providing their understanding of birth, death, rebirth, and fertility.

The second stage marks the beginnings of the mysteries, properly so-called, in which, following the Dorian invasions of the tenth or eleventh century B.C., the native population maintained these rites, already archaic, as an expression of their separate identity. Eventually they were forced to permit their political masters to be initiated into their rites, but they kept control of them in their own hands as hereditary priests.

The third stage arrived when the reputation of the cults spread beyond their native precincts, and candidates for initiation came from all over the Greek-speaking world. By this time the original meaning of the rites had been forgotten even by the priests, and the field was wide open for everyone, including a philosopher like Plato, to read into them his or her own meanings. These explanations, however, were not part of the rites, and it was the rites themselves that were protected by the requirement of absolute secrecy. The result is that we are badly informed about the exact nature of the rituals.

Many of the mysteries entered into a fourth phase in which a sort of evangelistic activity proclaimed the values of initiation through the Hellenistic world. This was frequently a kind of "hard sell" religious "hucksterism" designed to give the customers what they wanted.

The most famous of the mysteries were those of Demeter at Eleusis, a small town not far from Athens. Aristotle, like Plato an initiate, says:

> Those who are made initiates are not to learn but to experience, and so to bring about a true change in themselves.[45]

The myth of Demeter and her daughter Persephone, who was kidnapped by Hades and taken to his underground kingdom, and its significance for the alternation of the seasons and the rebirth of vegetation in the spring were well known by classical times. No secret information was given to the initiates, but they experienced the rite. They saw sacred objects and they performed ritual acts. From passing references in pagan authors and from denunciations by those who had abandoned the mysteries to accept Christianity, we can gain only the vaguest ideas of what actually happened.

The place of initiation was the *Telesterion* in Eleusis, a hall with many columns. After ritual purifications the initiates, their heads covered with cloth, were taken there and seated in a chair covered with animal skin. This was done at night to the accompaniment of torches. Clement of Alexandria quotes the formula that

was then recited by the initiates, but we are not sure
what it means:

> I fasted; I drank the draught; I took from the
> chest; having done my task; I placed in the basket,
> and from the basket into the chest.[46]

Eliade believes that the chest represented the
abode of the dead, and that to open the chest was symbolically to descend into Hades.[47] At the climactic moment of the rite the torches were extinguished, a curtain
raised, and the hierophant, the initiating priest, appeared with a box that he opened to reveal a single ripe
ear of grain.

In addition to this initiation rite there was the re-
curring celebration of a sort of passion-play in which
the myth of Demeter and Persephone was reenacted by
the initiates.

At the celebration of the mysteries, particularly
those of Dionysius, various forms of ecstatic behavior
were encouraged. Loud music and frenzied dancing
were frequently part of the rites. Sacred baths, sacred
meals, and sacred anointings were common; so were
various forms of sexual activity, at least in certain cults.
The technical term for the solemn rites or dramatic
reenactments of the myths that accompanied the celebrations was *orgia*. The English word "orgy" accurately reflects their nature. In fact, the Roman senate found
the rites of Bacchus so excessive that they forbade them
in 186 B.C.

There is no need to describe the other mysteries:
Isis and Osiris, Dionysius, the Great Mother, etc. These
were perceived to be the great competitors of Christianity by the Church Fathers. Clement of Alexandria,

in a famous passage, urges the devotees of the mystery cults to come to Christ and be initiated into the true mysteries. In this passage we can see the use that Christians were willing to make of the ideas of the mystery religions:

Then thou shalt have the vision of my God, and shalt be initiated into those holy mysteries, and shalt taste the joys that are hidden away in heaven, preserved for me "which neither ear hath heard nor have they entered into the heart" of any man. . . .

Come, thou frenzy-stricken one, not resting on thy wand, not wreathed with ivy! Cast off thy head-dress; cast off thy fawnskin; return to soberness! I will show thee the Word and the Word's mysteries, describing them according to thine own semblance of them. . . .

Christ, by whom the eyes of the blind see again shineth upon thee more brightly than the sun. Night shall flee from thee; fire shall fear thee; death shall depart from thee. Thou shalt see heaven, old man, though thou canst not see Thebes.

O truly sacred mysteries! O pure light! In the blaze of torches I have a vision of heaven and of God. I become holy by initiation. The Lord reveals the mysteries; He marks the worshiper with His seal, gives light to guide his way, and commends him, when he has believed, to the Father's care, where he is guarded for ages to come. These are the revels of my mysteries! If thou wilt, be thyself also initiated, and thou shalt dance with angels around

the unbegotten and imperishable and only true
God, the Word of God joining with us in our hymn
of praise.[48]

I believe we can see from this passage that, while
Christians were willing to make use of the terminology
of the mystery religions for evangelistic and catechetical purposes, they would have been unlikely to have
derived their rites from those of the mysteries.

Jewish Christianity

It was against this religious background that
Christianity made its way. It had no public sacrifices,
like the classical pagan rites of the Olympian gods, or
those of the Jerusalem Temple. It had no dramatic,
mysterious rites to intrigue the curious. It had only the
domestic celebration of a common meal.

The first Christians were, of course, Jews and were
accustomed to practice the rituals of the Jewish religion. They participated in the worship of the Temple
before its destruction in 70 A.D. They held Jewish religious meals, reinterpreted and given a new meaning by
Jesus. They also did something we have not previously
mentioned: they participated in the worship of the synagogue.

The synagogue is not at root a place of worship,
but a school. The rabbi is not a priest, but a teacher.
During the Babylonian exile (eighth century B.C.), when
it was impossible for the Jews to offer sacrifice in the
Jerusalem Temple, they met to study the religion they
were unable to practice and to pray. They began to see
the prayer that had accompanied the sacrifices of the
Temple as a substitute for the sacrifices themselves, and

although the Temple was rebuilt after the exile, more and more Jews began to see the study of the Scripture and the offering of prayer rather than sacrifice as the heart of worship.

We know that Jesus was called rabbi. The gospel tells us that He went regularly to the synagogue.[49] Synagogue worship was and is conducted by laymen. Any Jewish man may recite the prayers, read the Scriptures, and expound them. The rabbi preaches not because he is ordained, but because he is learned in the Scriptures and recognized as a teacher. St. Luke tells us that when Jesus visited the synagogue in Nazareth he read from the Book of Isaiah and expounded its meaning to the congregation.[50] Acts describes St. Paul preaching often in the synagogues.[51]

The tradition of the synagogue has become an integral part of the tradition of Christian worship that we have never abandoned in nearly two thousand years. The Liturgy of the Word of God, the solemn reading and exposition of the Scriptures, remains to the present an integral part of Christian worship.

The basic format of the morning worship of the synagogue will seem quite familiar to most Christians:[52]

1. *Invocation*, "Bless the Lord who is to be blessed."

2. *The Shema and its Benedictions*. The *shema* is the central Jewish profession of faith composed of Deuteronomy 6:4-9, 11:13-21; Numbers 15:37-41. It begins, "Hear, O Israel, the Lord our God, the Lord is one," and continues, "And you shall love the Lord your God with all your heart. . . ." In the synagogue liturgy it is preceded by two benedictions and followed by a third. They praise God for the creation of light (*Yotzer*), the love of God shown in the giving of the Torah (*Ahabah*), and the redemption from Egypt (*Geullah*). At least the

first is believed to be pre-Christian, and some scholars think all go back to the worship of the Temple. In the first century A.D. the Ten Commandments were read before the *shema*.

3. *Eighteen Benedictions*, called in Hebrew *Amidah* (standing). These are a series of prayers recited standing. The first three, called "praises," and the last three, called "thanksgivings," are the oldest. The middle section, petitions, were originally variable, and remained fluid for a long period.

4. *Reading from the Torah*. On sabbaths, holy days, and certain other occasions readings were added to the prayer.

5. *Reading from the Prophets*, at least on the sabbath in the time of Jesus.

6. *Homily*. Normally a rabbi or other teacher expounded the Scripture.

The psalms, which were originally sung in the Temple, were also a part of the synagogue service, perhaps sung in connection with the readings. They were also sung at meals, and upon other occasions.

We know that the earliest Christians regularly participated in the worship of the synagogue and Temple with their fellow Jews, in addition to performing their distinctively Christian rite, the common meal they celebrated on the Lord's Day as a "memorial" of their Lord. It is to this distinctive Christian rite that we now turn our attention.

NOTES

1. Justin Martyr, *First Apology* 64, 66, ed. Cyril C. Richardson, *Early Christian Fathers*, Library of Christian Classics 1 (Philadelphia: Westminster, 1953), pp. 285, 287.

2. E.g., Ribhard Reitzenstein, *Die hellenistische Mysterienreligionen* (Leipzig, 1910) or Wilhelm Bousset, *Kyrios Christos*, 2nd ed. (Göttingen, 1921).

3. Joseph Jungmann, *The Early Liturgy* (Notre Dame: University of Notre Dame Press, 1959), p. 153.

4. Odo Casel, *The Mystery of Christian Worship and Other Writings*, ed. Burkhard Neunheuser, tr. I. T. Hale (Westminister, Md.: Newman Press, 1962).

5. *Ibid.*, p. 34.

6. Louis Bouyer, *The Liturgy Revived* (Notre Dame: University of Notre Dame Press, 1964), pp. 11-27.

7. Cf. Frank Gavin, *The Jewish Antecedents of the Christian Sacraments* (London: S.P.C.K., 1928; reprinted New York: Ktav, 1969); W.O.E. Oesterly, *The Jewish Background of the Christian Liturgy* (Oxford: Oxford University Press, 1925); C. W. Dugmore, *The Influence of the Synagogue on the Divine Office* (Oxford: Oxford University Press, 1944; 2nd ed., Westminster: Faith Press, 1964).

8. Yerkes, *Sacrifice*, pp. 4f.

9. Bouyer, *Rite*, p. 86.

10. Matthew 26:17; Mark 14:12; Luke 22:7, 15.

11. I Corinthians 5:7-8.

12. Yerkes, *Sacrifice*, pp. 82-87.

13. Exodus 5:1.

14. *The Passover Haggadah*, ed. Nahum N. Glatzer (New York: Schocken Books, 1953, 1969), p. 23.

15. *Ibid.*, p. 51.

16. *The Draft Proposed Book of Common Prayer* (New York: Church Hymnal Corp., 1976), p. 289.

17. Exodus 12:1-11.

18. Hans-Joachim Kraus, *Worship in Israel*, tr. Geoffrey Buswell (Richmond: John Knox Press, 1966), p. 48.

19. Deuteronomy 16:5.

20. Yerkes, *Sacrifice*, pp. 97-109; 146-157.

21. *Ibid.*, pp. 126-146.

22. The ritual is in Leviticus 16.

23. *Haggadah*, pp. 17-19.

24. Mishna, *Berachoth* 8.1, ed. Philip Blackman, *Mishnayoth*, Vol. 1 (New York: Judaica Press, 1964), p. 65.

25. *The Authorized Daily Prayer Book of the United Hebrew Congregations of the British Empire*, tr. S. Singer,

14th ed. (London: Eyre and Spottiswoode, 1929), p. 124.

26. *Ibid.*

27. Gavin, *Jewish Antecedents*, p. 68.

28. I Corinthians 10:16.

29. Mishna, *Berachoth* 7.3, ed. Blackman, pp. 62f.

30. *Seder R. Amram Gaon*, ed. David Hedegard, Part I (Lund: Lindstedts, 1951), p. 147.

31. Louis Finkelstein, "The Birkat Ha-Mazon," *Jewish Quarterly Review*, n.s. 19 (1928-9), pp. 211-262. The text quoted is translated from the version printed in Anton Hänggi-Irmgard Paal, *Prex Eucharistica*, Specilegium Friburgense 12 (Fribourg: Editions Universitaires, 1968), pp. 9f.

32. Mark 14:23-24 RSV.

33. I Corinthians 10:20-21 RSV.

34. Yerkes, *Sacrifice*, p. 58.

35. *Ibid.*

36. *Phaedo* 69 C-D, tr. Harold R. Fowler, *Plato* 1, Loeb Classical Library, (Cambridge: Harvard University Press, 1953) p. 241.

37. *Phaedrus* 250 C-D, tr. Fowler, p. 485.

38. Casel, *Mystery*, p. 54.

39. *Ibid.*, p. 53.

40. *Ibid.*, p. 45.

41. E.g. Reginald H. Fuller, "Christian Initiation in the New Testament," *Made, Not Born*, ed. Murphy Center for Liturgical Research (Notre Dame: University of Notre Dame Press, 1976), p. 17.

42. Cf. Fuller's treatment in *Made, Not Born*, pp. 18-24.

43. George Every, *The Baptismal Sacrifice*, Studies in Ministry and Worship (London: S.C.M. Press, 1959), pp. 21f.

44. Bouyer, *Rite*, p. 126f. Cf. his entire exposition in the chapter "Pagan Mysteries and Christian Sacraments," pp. 123-150; also Jungmann, *Early Liturgy*, Ch. 12, "Pagan and Christian Mysteries," pp. 152-163.

45. Aristotle, Fragment 15, cited in Casel, *Mystery*, p. 112.

46. Clement of Alexandria, *Exhortation to the Greeks (Protrepticus)* 18, tr. G. W. Butterworth, *Clement of Alexandria*, Loeb Classical Library (Cambridge: Harvard University Press, 1960), p. 43.

47. Eliade, *Rites*, pp. 110f.

48. Clement, *Protrepticus* 92-93, tr. Butterworth, pp. 253-257.

49. Luke 4:16.

50. Luke 4:16-30.

51. Acts 13:14-43; 14:1; 17:1-3, 10, 17; 18:4, 18-20; 19:8.

52. Dugmore, *Influence*, pp. 11-25.

3

Origin of the Christian Liturgy

Christianity is, of course, more than a ritual; and the Apostolic Church did not simply celebrate a ritual meal, it proclaimed a gospel. We hear St. Peter proclaiming it in the Acts of the Apostles:

God anointed Jesus of Nazareth with the Holy Spirit and with power. . . . He went about doing good and healing all that were oppressed by the devil, for God was with him. And we are witnesses to all that he did both in the country of the Jews and in Jerusalem. They put him to death by hanging him on a tree; but God raised him on the third day and made him manifest; not to all the people but to us who were chosen by God as witnesses, who ate and drank with him after he rose from the dead. And he commanded us to testify that he is the one ordained by God to be judge of the living and the dead. To him all the prophets bear witness that every one who believes in him receives forgiveness of sins through his name.[1]

The words are undoubtedly those of the author of Acts and not of the Apostle Peter, but the proclamation is the core of the apostolic preaching. The Christian "myth" is not the recounting of primeval events accomplished by the gods before the dawn of time that are reactualized in the celebration of the rites. The apostolic preaching is rooted in historical events that took place in Palestine in the first half of the first century A.D. These decisive events had taken place but once and could not be repeated. It was this teaching that transformed the traditional Jewish rituals they still used. They read the Hebrew Scriptures in the light of their assurance that "Jesus Christ is Lord."[2] Even the familiar words of the Twenty-third Psalm took on new meaning, for Jesus was for them the Lord who was their Good Shepherd.

The Lord's Supper

It was this revelation of Jesus as Lord that transformed the celebration of the traditional Jewish common meal into a new and different thing, the Lord's Supper, or the Eucharist. On the night before Jesus died, he had sat at the head of the table with his disciples and celebrated a traditional Jewish meal. What he said and did gave to the fellowship meal a radically different meaning. He took two items from the ordinary table ritual, the breaking of bread at the beginning and the blessing over a cup of wine at the end, and gave them a profoundly new level of meaning. "This is my Body." "This is my Blood." "Do this for the remembrance of me." Immediately after supper he went out to his death. From then on, whenever his disciples pronounced the blessing over the bread and the cup at their meals they would "proclaim the Lord's death until he comes."[3] In the words of Gregory Dix:

From what He said and did at the Supper, His *chaburah* (fellowship) came to understand that death to be, not the scandal of a death under the curse of God which it appeared, but the offering of His own Body and Blood as the inaugural sacrifice of the "New Covenant" by the Messianic High-Priest-Prophet-King.[4]

The Lord's Supper enabled the disciples to see the death of Jesus not as an execution, but as a part of a sacrifice that was manifestly accepted by God when he raised him from the dead. If we look back at the outline of a sacrifice[4a] we can see what Jesus did. He offered himself as the victim, identifying himself with the human race by becoming a man and living a human life. Then he laid down his life, a life perfectly united to God, out of love for his fellowmen. The Epistle to the Hebrews speaks of Jesus as the great high priest who carried his offering not into the Temple in Jerusalem, but into heaven itself, and poured out his own blood to purify human uncleanness before the throne of God, where he remains forever offering intercessions for us. He completed his sacrifice by providing, at the Last Supper, that we might have a share in it, in the usual way in which sacrifices are shared, by participating in the common meal, the banquet on the flesh of the victim that unites the worshipers with one another and with God. To eat and drink at the Lord's Supper, then, unites Christians in a specific way with Jesus, God and man, for he is our food, our host, our Savior, and our priest. The "New Covenant in his blood" sets up a new people, a fellowship of God and men, which is symbolized and celebrated in the meal.

What was new for Christians was not the ritual of the Lord's Supper. It was the same meal-ritual they had always celebrated as Jews. It was their understanding of it. A new meaning had been added to the old. The Epistle to the Hebrews tells us that what was only symbolized in the Jewish rites was fulfilled in Christ.[4b] The command "Do this" did not involve them in doing anything they would not have done anyway. The apostles were observant Jews and they would never have eaten without blessing the bread and the cup. What it does is to give them a new understanding of what they are doing. The mystery of Christ's death and resurrection is made present again in the celebration of the Supper. Just as the Passover ritual tells the Jew that he must consider himself to have come out of Egypt, the Lord's Supper renews for Christians the saving act of God in Christ.

A First-Century Celebration

We may imagine a group of first-century Christians gathered in the home of one of their number. It is a Saturday night. They have spent the sabbath in the synagogue with their fellow Jews, hearing the Old Testament read and expounded, singing the psalms, and reciting the benedictions and prayers. Now it is past sunset and the sabbath is over and they are gathered to do their distinctively Christian thing in celebration of the Lord's Day, the day on which Jesus rose from the dead. What do they do?

They *do* the same thing Jews always do on Friday night when they celebrate the sabbath, the same thing they themselves had probably done the previous evening: they eat supper gathered around a well-set table. The apostle or bishop says the blessing, breaks the bread, and passes it around the table, and he reminds them that they do this as the memorial of Jesus Christ. Then they eat. They talk, as they have always talked at formal meals, about the Law of God, and about works of charity, but now they also speak of Jesus the Messiah, and his resurrection. Perhaps someone tells a story of his life, or retells a story he told. They may read a letter from another group of Christians, like those of St. Paul we find in the New Testament.

At the end of the meal they sing psalms, and the "cup of blessing" is brought out. Over it their leader sings the Great Thanksgiving, giving thanks, as always, for the food, and probably also for God's new people, the Christian Church. Certainly he gives thanks for Jesus Christ himself and offers his prayer in his Name.

We are fortunate that a set of prayers has been preserved in an early Christian document called *Didache*, The Teaching of the Twelve Apostles, which appears to be exactly the kind of things Jewish Christians of the first century would have said:

> *Now about the Eucharist: This is how to give thanks.*
> *First in connection with the cup:*
>
> We thank you, our Father, for the holy vine of David, your child, which you have revealed through Jesus, your child. To you be glory forever.
>
> *Then in connection with the broken bread:*
>
> We thank you, our Father, for life and knowledge which you have revealed through Jesus, your child. To you be glory forever.

As this bread was scattered over the hills and then was brought together and made one, so let your Church be brought together from the ends of the earth into your Kingdom. For yours is the glory and the power through Jesus Christ forever.

After you have finished your meal, say grace in this way:

We thank you, holy Father, for your sacred name which you have lodged in our hearts, and for knowledge and faith and immortality which you have revealed through Jesus, your child. To you be glory forever.

Almighty Master, you have created everything for the sake of your name, and have given men food and drink to enjoy that they may thank you. But to us you have given spiritual food and drink and eternal life through Jesus, your child.

Above all we thank you that you are mighty. To you be glory forever. Remember, Lord, your Church, to save it from all evil and to make it perfect by your love. Make it holy, and gather it together from the four winds into your Kingdom which you have made ready for it. For yours is the power and the glory forever.[5]

Jewish scholars who have compared these prayers with the Jewish table prayers we discussed in the last chapter describe them as Christian adaptations of the Jewish prayers.[6] The similarity is striking.

First there appears to be a blessing over the *kiddush* cup, although that may be a misinterpretation of the purpose of the prayer.[7] Then follows the prayer of blessing for the breaking of the bread. It is substantive-ly longer than the Jewish bread blessing, but this was certainly the most significant act for Christians, and they had more to say about it. After the meal, the long grace over the cup of blessing is obviously modeled on the three paragraphs of the Jewish grace.

The second paragraph of this prayer, giving thanks for the food, corresponds to the opening paragraph of the Jewish grace, but goes on to thank God for the spir-itual food and drink of the Body and Blood of Christ which give us eternal life. The first paragraph is a spiri-tualization of the second paragraph of the Jewish prayer, substituting thanks for the gift of God's name, knowledge, faith, and immortality, for thanks for the good land. The third paragraph thanks God for the new Israel of the Church Universal, as the Jewish form gives thanks for Israel, Jerusalem, and the Temple.

The eucharistic prayers of the *Didache* end with the acclamation found also at the end of I Corinthians and the Book of Revelation, "Marantha! Our Lord, come."[8] It is the distinctive prayer of the early Chris-tians looking for the coming again of Christ in glory, and it gives a future orientation to their worship. Dr. Marianne Micks has described the Christian past as "a time when worshipers were eagerly looking forward,"[9] and commented:

Insofar as Christian worship remains rooted in its own history and faithful to its ancient liturgy, it not only recalls the past but eagerly strains toward the future.[10]

Certainly the references to the gathering of the Church into the Kingdom and the eschatological cry

"Maranatha!" show that the Christians who used these prayers were indeed looking not only back to the life of Christ, but forward to his expected return. It is this content that makes the common meal of the early Christians radically different from the Jewish meal. The ritual is the same. The prayers are based on Jewish models, but the content has changed. God is addressed as "Our Father," following Jesus' example, and the prayers are offered "through Jesus, your child," as a memorial, or *anamnesis*, of what he has done and will do. The mighty act of God in Christ has decisively separated this new meal, the Lord's Supper of the New Covenant, from the sabbath meal of the Old Covenant. The ritual is the same, but the inner meaning, the thing signified, as traditional Christian theology calls it, is totally different.

The Eucharist Becomes a "Service"

It was at this point in Christian history that the most profound change in the external rite of Christian worship took place, and we have almost no evidence as to how it happened. Somehow, the Lord's Supper was separated from the meal and acquired the format with which we are familiar: that of a service of worship. What happened is clear, but we do not know exactly when, where, or why the change was made. The meal ceased to be eaten. The blessing of the bread at its beginning was joined to the blessing of the cup at the end to form what Gregory Dix called the fourfold "shape of the liturgy": we take bread and wine, we bless them, we break the bread, we distribute and eat them.[11] This is the uniform shape of the Christian Eucharist after the second century. Already in 150 A.D. at Rome Justin Martyr describes the Christian Eucharist this way:

> On the day called Sunday there is a meeting in one place of those who live in the cities or the country, and the memoirs of the apostles or the writings of the prophets are read as long as time permits. When the reader has finished, the president in a discourse urges and invites us to the imitation of these noble things. Then we all stand up together and offer prayers. And, as we said before, the president similarly sends up prayers and thanksgivings to the best of his ability, and the congregation assents, saying Amen; the distribution, and reception of the consecrated elements by each one, takes place and they are sent to the absent by the deacons.[12]

We can recognize the familiar outline of the Eucharist as it is still celebrated. The blessing of the bread and the cup has been joined to a service of Scripture reading and prayers which is based upon the worship of the synagogue. The question is, why was the change made?

Perhaps there is a hint in St. Paul's criticism of the Christians at Corinth:

> When you meet together, it is not the Lord's Supper that you eat. For in eating each one goes ahead with his own meal, and one is hungry and another is drunk. What! Do you not have houses to eat and drink in? Or do you despise the church of God and humiliate those who have nothing?[13]

St. Paul is certainly describing a real meal, and it may be that the abuses he describes were not unique to Corinth. The Greeks did not have the Jewish tradition of the religious meal in which St. Paul and the Jerusalem Christians had been brought up. Perhaps the tradition of the sacred "orgy" had been carried over from the mystery religions. Certainly this was what the pagans believed of the early Christians.

Another possible clue is found in the letter that Pliny the Younger wrote to the Emperor Trajan, describing what he had learned of the customs of the Christians in Bithynia:

> It was their habit on a fixed day to assemble before daylight and recite by turns a form of words to Christ as a god: and . . . they bound themselves with an oath, not for any crime, but not to commit theft or robbery or adultery, not to break their word, and not to deny a deposit when demanded. After this was done their custom was to depart, and to meet again to take food, but ordinary and harmless food; and even this (they said) they had given up after my edict, by which in accordance with your commands I had forbidden the existence of clubs.[14]

This letter, written by one with no personal knowledge of Christianity, raises more questions than it answers. What is clear is that the Christians had been accustomed to gather both before daylight and again for a meal in the evening, but that the objection of the Roman government to evening meetings of "clubs" had caused them to abandon their evening gathering. It is possible that this letter is describing a sort of synagogue service in the morning, with the recitation of the Ten Commandments and prayers, followed by an evening meeting for Eucharist. The prohibition on evening meetings would then be the cause of their joining the essential rites of the Lord's Supper, the blessing and eating of the bread and wine, to their morning service.

The letter has also been interpreted to mean that the Christians were already celebrating the Eucharist in the morning, the "form of words," *carmen* in Latin, being take to mean not a hymn or psalm, but the opening dialogue of the eucharistic prayer. In this case, the evening supper would have been an ordinary supper. We know that such meals, called *agape*, were held by Christians in the third century.[15] In fact, they lasted into the fifth century as a sort of charity supper given by the church for the poor.[16] This persistence of the *agape* as a fellowship meal long after its separation from the Eucharist is an example of the reluctance of people to abandon religious rituals, even after the original reason for performing them no longer exists. The rite itself acquires a sort of durability, even when its meaning has completely changed.

However the evidence of Pliny is correctly understood, we can only guess about the details of the separation of the Eucharist from the meal that was its original context. Certainly the Lord's Supper that St. Paul knew in Corinth was an actual meal, and the Eucharist described by Justin Martyr was not. For some reason, the ritual acts over the bread and cup were separated from the meal itself. The two blessings were joined into a single prayer, and the Eucharist took the shape it has kept ever since.

The Sunday Eucharist

Justin describes the Eucharist on Sundays as joined to a type of synagogue service. It is probable that Christians had begun to conduct such services themselves after they were expelled from the Jewish synagogues. Pliny may be describing such a morning service. Justin, on the other hand, does know the Eucharist not so connected to a service of readings. The Eucharist he describes following the celebration of baptism begins with the prayers of the people, and continues with the offertory.[17] The *Apostolic Tradition*, about sixty years later, describes the Eucharist at an ordination as well as at a baptism as beginning with the offertory.[18] The most reasonable explanation for this would seem to be that the eucharistic rite, once the meal had been eliminated, was too short to celebrate alone, and it was attached to some other service, either an ordination, or a baptism, or the service of readings and prayers.

With Justin's account we are again on firm ground. He gives us our first clear account of Christian rituals outside the New Testament. Justin was a philosopher who had embraced Christianity and tried to commend it to the Hellenistic world as the true philosophy. His *First Apology* is in the form of an open letter to the Emperor Antoninus Pius, defending the Christians against the common charges of antistate activity, magic, cannibalism, and incest that were leveled against them. In addition to the Sunday Eucharist, Justin describes the Eucharist that concludes the baptismal rite. In the text of his treatise it precedes the description of the Sunday service, and is in some ways more detailed. As we have already said, it does not include the readings and sermon that Justin describes for Sundays:

> We, however, after thus washing the one who has
> been convinced and signified his assent, lead him
> to those who are called brethren, where they are
> assembled. Then they earnestly offer common
> prayers for themselves and for the one who has
> been illuminated and all others everywhere, that
> we may be made worthy, having learned the truth,
> to be found in deed good citizens and keepers of
> what is commanded, so that we may be saved with
> eternal salvation. On finishing the prayers we greet
> each other with a kiss. Then bread and a cup of
> water and mixed wine are brought to the president
> of the brethren and he, taking them, sends up
> praise and glory to the Father of the universe
> through the name of the Son and of the Holy
> Spirit, and offers thanksgiving at some length that
> we have been deemed worthy to receive these
> things from him. When he has finished the prayers
> and the thanksgiving, the whole congregation pres-
> ent assents, saying "Amen." "Amen" in the He-
> brew language means, "So be it." When the presi-
> dent has given thanks and the whole congregation
> has assented, those whom we call deacons give to
> each of those present a portion of the consecrated
> bread and wine and water, and they take it to the
> absent.[19]

If we consider both of Justin's accounts, we find he
describes a service similar to that celebrated by most
Christians today:

1. Readings from the Scripture, including the gospel ("the memoirs of the apostles").

2. Homily or sermon.
3. Common Prayers.
4. Kiss of Peace
5. Offertory
6. Eucharistic   prayer,   with   congregational "Amen."
7. Distribution of communion.

The Eucharistic Prayer

Justin seems to be telling us that the "president of the brethren" composed the lengthy prayer of thanksgiving, or eucharistic prayer, "to the best of his ability." We might note that the people in whose name he prays assent vocally to the prayer with the Hebrew word we still use for the purpose, "Amen." If Justin does mean that the president composed the prayer himself, then we shall not be able to find a "text" of the eucharistic prayer from this period. There is every reason to believe that the individual Christian bishops did compose their own prayers, according to a commonly accepted outline. This was apparently also contemporary Jewish practice. The themes of the prayers were fixed, but the actual wording was the work of the one reciting the prayer.

The earliest Christian eucharistic prayer we do possess is about sixty years later than Justin, and it is provided for the use of a new bishop upon the occasion of his ordination.[20] Even this written prayer, however, was accompanied by a warning:

Let the bishop give thanks in the way we have said.

It is not at all necessary that he say the exact words that we have given, as though being careful to say them by heart, in giving thanks to God; but let each one pray according to his ability. If one can pray at length with a solemn prayer, it is good. If, however, one, when he prays, prays a more modest prayer, none shall prevent him, as long as he prays what is sound in the right faith.[21]

The source of this prayer is *The Apostolic Tradition* of Hippolytus, probably the most important document on the life and worship of the early Church to have survived. We believe it was composed in Rome in about the years 210 A.D. by Hippolytus, a conservative reactionary, who wished to recall the Roman Church to its apostolic tradition, in the fact of what he considered dangerous novelties being introduced into its life and worship. The treatise itself is a complete manual for church life, probably written as unsolicited advice for a newly elected bishop. What the author does is to present a sort of idealized picture of a Christian congregation in the "good old days," which he identifies with the apostolic tradition of the Church, and clearly suggests that it should be a model for the Church of his contemporaries.[22]

Hippolytus' prayer, which he himself considered only a model, has found its way into the *Worship Supplement* of the Lutheran Church—Missouri Synod,[23] and served as the source for Eucharistic Prayer II of the Roman Sacramentary[24] and, to a lesser extent, for Eucharistic Prayer B of the *Draft Proposed Book of Common Prayer.*[25] It is significant because of its early date and its similarity in structure and content to later, lengthier prayers. It is still, in fact, a useful model for the composition of eucharistic prayers:

> *Let the deacons present to him (the bishop) the oblations and let him, laying his hands upon them with all the presbytery, give thanks and say:*
> The Lord be with you.

> *And let all say:*
> And with your spirit.
> Lift up your hearts.
> We have to the Lord.
> Let us give thanks to the Lord.
> Worthy and right.

> *And let him continue thus:*
> We give you thanks, O God, through your beloved child Jesus Christ, whom in these last days you have sent to us a Savior and Redeemer and Messenger of your will, who is your inseparable Word, through whom you created all things, and whom, in your good pleasure, you sent from heaven into the womb of the Virgin, and who dwelt in ·her womb and was made man and shown to be your Son, born of the Holy Spirit and the Virgin.

> When he had accomplished your will and gained for you a holy people, he stretched forth his hands to suffer, that by his passion he might set free those who have trusted in you.

> When he was betrayed to his freely chosen passion, that he might destroy death and break the chains of the devil and tread hell underfoot and enlighten the righteous and fix the limit and manifest the resurrection, he took bread and, giving thanks to

you, said: Take, eat, this is my body which is broken for you.

Likewise also the cup, saying: This is my blood which is shed for you. Whenever you do this you make my memorial.

Remembering therefore his death and resurrection, we offer you the bread and the cup, giving thanks to you that you have made us worthy to stand before you and minister to you.

And we ask that you send your Holy Spirit upon the oblation of the holy church, that all who partake of these holy things being gathered into one may be filled with the Holy Spirit, for the strengthening of their faith in the truth, that we may praise and glorify you through your child Jesus Christ, through whom to you be glory and honor, Father, Son, and Holy Spirit, in your holy church, now and forever. Amen.[26]

The content of the prayer is largely the core of the apostolic preaching, the same events that found a place in the Apostles' Creed. The prayer also follows the general order of the Creed, beginning with the praise of the Creator, moving through the incarnation, passion and resurrection of the Son, to a prayer for the coming of the Holy Spirit upon the Church.

The prayer of Hippolytus, like contemporary eucharistic prayers, begins with a dialogue similar to that which precedes the Jewish grace after meals. Like Justin's "Amen," it involves the entire congregation in the prayer which one member is saying in its name. It begins with thanksgiving, or eucharist, and ends with the praise of the Trinity.

The common outline this prayer shares with other eucharistic prayers in this:

1. Thanksgiving to God, or eucharist properly so-called. Thanks are given first for creation and then for redemption through Jesus Christ.

2. Institution Narrative. Usually this forms the conclusion of the thanksgiving for God's mighty acts in Christ, giving thanks that he took bread and gave it to his disciples.

3. *Anamnesis*. This is the Greek word for "memorial" and has become the technical term for a prayer that moves from recalling what Christ did to what we are doing. "Remembering his death and resurrection, we offer you the bread and the cup."

4. *Epiclesis*. Like *anamnesis*, this is a Greek word. It means "calling down" and is the technical term for a prayer asking God to send down the Holy Spirit upon the bread and wine, or upon the gathered praying church.

5. *Doxology*. Another, more familiar Greek word. It means "giving glory" and is the technical term for the ascription of praise to Father, Son, and Holy Spirit with which Christian prayers have traditionally closed.

Later prayers frequently expand these elements, but all are normally found in them. At an early date the *Sanctus*, the hymn Isaiah heard the seraphim singing before the throne of God,[27] became a regular part of the prayer. Usually it separated the opening praises and thanksgivings from the specific recounting of the events of Christ's death and resurrection, or the thanksgiving for creation from the thanksgiving for redemption. In the Middle Ages Christians began to think of the eucharistic prayer, the *canon missae*, as beginning after the *Sanctus*. To some extent this was because the illuminators of missals were accustomed to use the capital T with which the prayer following the *Sanctus* (*Te igitur*) began, to illuminate with a full-page illustration of the crucifixion. This, of course, put the first part of the prayer on an earlier page. This prayer of Hippolytus makes it clear that the prayer begins with the dialogue "Lift up your hearts." The praise and thanksgiving in what we are accustomed to call the Preface are an integral part of the prayer. This should have been clear to the users of the Latin liturgy, since the prayer after the *Sanctus* continued "Therefore, most merciful Father . . ." clearly referring to the praise and thanksgiving that had gone before.

The *Sanctus*, known in Hebrew as the *Qedusha*, is also a part of the Jewish liturgy of the synagogue. It is not known whether it was taken over by Christians from Jewish usage, or whether it is simply a parallel development of the two liturgies.

In most liturgies the *epiclesis*, the invocation of the Holy Spirit, is considerably expanded. Frequently the expansion refers to the purpose of the descent of the Spirit upon the bread and wine. The Byzantine liturgy of St. Basil, for example, prays the Father:

> . . . to send your All-Holy Spirit upon us and upon these gifts here present, and to bless them, and consecrate and proclaim this Bread the precious Body of our Lord and God and Savior Jesus Christ, and this Cup the precious Blood of our Lord and Savior Jesus Christ, poured out for the life of the world.[28]

This is, of course, more specific than any prayer for consecration as early as Hippolytus, but Justin

Martyr in 150 A.D. was already able to say of the "food we call eucharist":

> We do not receive these things as common bread or common drink: but as Jesus Christ our Saviour being incarnate by God's word took flesh and blood for our salvation, so also we have been taught that the food consecrated by the word of prayer which comes from him, from which our flesh and blood are nourished by transformation, is the flesh and blood of that incarnate Jesus.[29]

The "word of prayer which comes from him" is apparently the eucharistic prayer which, as Justin goes on to tell his readers, derives from our Lord's institution.

Another way in which the *epiclesis* is expanded is by enlarging the mention of "the holy church." *Apostolic Tradition* prays for all who partake, and other liturgies include a considerable body of intercessions for the Church here, and throughout the world. The fellowship of the saints on earth with those in eternal glory also finds expression here, and the intercessions sometimes become the longest part of the prayer. The prayer for the Church leads naturally to prayers for bishops, priests, deacons, and lay people, living and departed, all of whom are included in the Church upon whose offering the Holy Spirit is called down.

If we wish to reconstruct the Sunday service of the second-century Church, we can follow Justin's outline and use Hippolytus' eucharistic prayer. The result is a service clearly recognizable as a "stripped down" version of contemporary eucharistic liturgies. The gospel, the sermon, the prayers of the people, the offertory, the eucharistic prayer, the communion—all the essentials are there. We can see here the descent of our present liturgy from the worship of the synagogue and the action of Christ at the Last Supper.

Rites of Christian Initiation

Christian initiation is not one rite, it is a process that introduces the novice, technically called a *catechumen,* into the fellowship of the Christian Church. Like the primitive initiations we examined, or the initiations into the mystery religions, it involves both ritual acts and the imparting of oral teaching. In modern times it has, of course, been possible to give inquirers books to read, but traditionally the instruction of new Christians has been oral, and the bishops and other ministers of the Church have taken a prominent place in the process.

The *Didache*, probably our earliest description of baptism outside the New Testament, begins its account, "Give public instruction on all these points."[30] Justin Martyr says:

> Those who are persuaded and believe that the things we teach and say are true, and promise that they can live accordingly, are instructed to pray and beseech God with fasting for the remission of their past sins, while we pray and fast along with them.[31]

Apostolic Tradition describes a three-year period of instruction.[32] From the fourth century we have preserved the catechetical instructions of St. Ambrose, St.

Chrysostom, St. Cyril of Jerusalem, and Bishop Theodore of Mopsuestia, which they gave during Lent to the candidates for Easter baptism.[33]

Of this initiatory process, the celebration of the sacraments of baptism and Eucharist formed the climax, but it was not the only ritual occasion. As the Church developed during the first four centuries it integrated its initiation rites into its developing liturgical year. The period of final preparation of the candidates was fixed as the forty days of Lent; baptism was celebrated at the Great Vigil of Easter; and the instruction of the newly baptized in the meaning of the sacraments, which is called *mystagogy*, took place during what we call Easter Week. The inner meaning of Christian initiation is, of course, participation in the death and rising again of Jesus, and its celebration became the Church's chief celebration of the *pascha*, the paschal mystery of Christ.

In the rites of Christian initiation those who were outside the Christian fellowship were united with Christ and through him with the people of God, the Church. The sacrament of baptism is the means of this union. As St. Paul wrote to the Romans:

Do you not know that all of us who have been baptized into Christ Jesus were baptized into his death? We were buried therefore with him by baptism into death, so that as Christ was raised from the dead by the glory of the Father, we too might walk in newness of life.

For if we have been united with him in a death like his, we shall certainly be united with him in a resurrection like his. We know that our old self was crucified with him so that the sinful body might be destroyed, and we might no longer be enslaved to sin. For he who died is free from sin. But if we have died with Christ, we believe that we shall also live with him. For we know that Christ being raised from the dead will never die again; death no longer has dominion over him. The death he died he died to sin, once for all, but the life he lives, he lives to God. So you also must consider yourselves dead to sin and alive to God in Christ Jesus.[34]

This is the language of initiation. It is language that Greeks who had been initiated into the mystery religions would understand. In ritual terms, baptism is a death, followed by a rebirth or resurrection. The candidates go down into the water and die. They are covered with the waters as the earth was covered with the life-destroying waters of the Flood. But, like all life, they rise newborn from the waters. In Eliade's phrase,

The novice emerges from the ordeal with a totally different being from that which he possessed before his initiation; he has become another.[35]

St. Paul said, "It is no longer I who live, but Christ who lives in me."[36] Baptism is an initiation rite that makes us members of a new community of which Christ is the head:

You are a chosen race, a royal priesthood, a holy nation, God's own people, that you may declare the wonderful deeds of him who called you out of darkness into his marvelous light. Once you were no people but now you are God's people; once you had not received mercy but now you have received mercy.[37]

This passage is from the First Epistle of St. Peter, which may itself have been a part of an early baptismal rite.[38]

Our earliest full description of Christian initiation is in *Apostolic Tradition.* We can supplement this with other sources, mostly references in sermons, and discover a common outline of a rite of initiation that lasted from at least the beginning of the third century well into the Middle Ages. The rite has the structure of initiation rites, as van Gennep describes them.[39] First there is a rite of separation, admission to the catechumenate, then a liminal period of intensive instruction, and finally the sacramental rites of baptism and Eucharist incorporate the new members into the body of Christ, the Church. The ritual pattern of the baptism itself was the account of the baptism of Christ in the synoptic gospels:

In those days Jesus came from Nazareth of Galilee and was baptized by John in the Jordan. And when he came up out of the water, immediately he saw the heavens opened and the Spirit descending upon him like a dove; and a voice came from heaven, "Thou art my beloved Son, with thee I am well pleased."[40]

This account describes three actions: (1) Jesus goes down into the water with John; (2) when he comes up, he sees the Spirit descend; and (3) he hears the voice of the Father proclaim his Sonship. It is this pattern that most Christian baptismal rites reproduce.

The Catechumenate

Apostolic Tradition says that those who first come "to hear the word" are examined before the "teachers" as to their reasons for desiring to become Christians.[41] This was also the tradition of the rabbis concerning those who wished to become Jews.[42] It was by no means a perfunctory examination. Candidates were presented by sponsors who were required to testify to their *bona fides*; an examination was made of their manner of life; and certain trades and occupations considered to be incompatible with the profession of Christianity were prohibited to them. Eventually this became a formal ceremony of admission to the catechumenate. Hippolytus tells us that catechumens were "to hear the word" for three years, but that what was significant was not the time but the conversion of the candidate to a Christian manner of life.[43] We know that often catechumens did not move on to actual preparation for baptism for many years. St. Augustine is an outstanding example.

The suggestion is sometimes made today that this practice should be revived, that infants should be admitted to the catechumenate and be permitted "to hear the word" until they are themselves able and willing to request baptism. There were undoubtedly many instances of this happening in the fourth and fifth centuries, but it was never the deliberate policy of the Church. Infants were included among those whom *Apostolic Tradition* describes as receiving baptism,[44] and the purpose of the long catechumenate was to produce a decisive change in life-style in converts who had not grown up in the Judeo-Christian ethic we take for granted. A great deal of ordinary social life in the second and third centuries was so intertwined with pagan worship that a potential convert needed a substantial period to adjust to a "Christian" way of living.

During this liminal period the catechumens were present for the reading and exposition of the Scripture in the Christian assembly. They then prayed separately from the baptized Christians and were dismissed by their teacher with a blessing.[45]

As the time approached for the celebration of baptism, the candidates were chosen after another examination of their lives.[46] This group, which was separated from the other catechumens, came to be called the "elect" or the "seekers." We have a detailed description of this enrollment of the "seekers" in fourth century Jerusalem by a Western visitor, the nun Egeria. She tells us that the names of those who wished to be enrolled for baptism had to be given in before the first day of Lent. The actual enrollment and examination had become a solemn ceremony, presided over by the bishop, sitting in his chair with his presbyters and deacons standing behind him.

The candidates were brought forward one at a time with their sponsors. The bishop asked their neighbors direct questions about their manner of life. He then either told them to amend their ways and come another year or himself wrote their names in the register. In the second century the ceremony was probably not so formal, but it marked a definite entrance into a new status. As "seekers" the candidates received daily instruction and exorcism, and since the period of this instruction corresponds to what we call Lent, we have here the beginnings of the practice of a daily service during Lent. Egeria tells us that in Jerusalem the "seekers" sat around the bishop's chair in a circle, that their sponsors attended the daily instructions with them, and that many of the faithful also came to listen.[47] *Apostolic Tradition* implies that others attended, for it says in its general instructions to the faithful:

> If there is an instruction in the Word everyone ought to go there to hear the Word of God for the strengthening of his soul.[48]

Sacraments of Initiation

The actual preparation for baptism began on Maundy Thursday. The "seekers" were told to wash and prepare themselves for baptism by fasting all day Friday and Saturday.[49] Originally there was no suggestion that Good Friday was the day of the crucifixion, Holy Saturday the day of the burial, or Maundy Thursday the day of the Last Supper. The *pascha* was a single celebration in the night between Holy Saturday and Easter, preceded by two days of fasting. The fast is described by all of the earliest writers as of two days *before baptism*. Originally the candidates and the baptizers fasted, then the whole Church joined in the fasting. It was after the legalization of Christianity in the fourth century that the historicization of the days of Holy Week took place. It began in Jerusalem and was one of the unique things the pilgrim Egeria had to tell her sisters back home about the Jerusalem Church.[50]

On Holy Saturday the bishop met with the candidates and prayed over them. At a later period we know that on this occasion the candidates recited individually the creed they had been taught during their instruction as a prebaptismal profession of Christian faith.[51]

The Paschal night is spent in vigil, listening to

reading and instruction. This is the Great Vigil of Easter. The Bible readings and instructions would be a sort of summary of the teaching the candidates had received. We cannot be certain what passages of Scripture were actually read, but certain ones occur on so many of the oldest lists that we may reasonably conjecture that the account of the creation and fall from Genesis, the Exodus account of the crossing of the Red Sea, and the story of the binding of Isaac from Genesis 22 were among them.

At cockcrow, the bishop led the "seekers" to the baptistry, which was usually a separate room from that in which the Eucharist was celebrated, one with a sunken pool and a source of flowing water.[52] The bishop blessed the water and the holy oil to be used in the rite. The candidates removed their clothing, and standing before a presbyter renounced the devil. The presbyter anointed them with the "oil of exorcism," and they went down into the water.

A deacon accompanied each candidate into the water. The baptizing priest, who may have been either the bishop himself or one of the presbyters, asked each one, laying his hand upon him:

Do you believe in God the Father Almighty?

The candidate responded, "I believe," and was baptized.

A second time the priest asked:

Do you believe in Christ Jesus, the Son of God, who was born by the Holy Spirit of the Virgin Mary and crucified under Pontius Pilate, died, and rose again the third day alive from the dead, and ascended to heaven and sits at the right hand of the Father, and who will come to judge the living and the dead?

A second time the candidate replied, "I believe," and was baptized.

A third time he asked:

Do you believe in the Holy Spirit and the holy church and the resurrection of the flesh?

And the third time, "I believe," and the washing.

When each one came up out of the water he was anointed in the name of Jesus Christ with the "oil of thanksgiving" by the presbyter. The "oil of thanksgiving" is the oil over which the bishop has given thanks. It is also called *myron* and *chrism*. The newly baptized then dressed and entered the church where the congregation awaited them. The bishop prayed over them imposing his hands, and signed each one on the forehead with the holy oil, greeting the new brother or sister with the kiss of peace.

The newly baptized were now incorporated into the Christian fellowship and immediately joined with the faithful in the prayers and in the exchange of the peace, both of which they had previosly been forbidden to do. They also offered their *prosphora*, their gifts of bread and wine, which were brought by the deacons to the bishop were consecrated them. Finally, they joined with the rest of the Church in receiving Easter communion. Upon this occasion the newly baptized received also a cup of water and one of milk and honey, symbolizing their entry into the promised land, and their first feeding as newborn Christians.

Structure and Meaning of the Rite

As we have said, the ritual pattern is that of the baptism of Christ. The candidates go down into the water, as Jesus did in Jordan. When they come up they are anointed with the chrism, as Jesus was anointed with the Holy Spirit. The bishop lays on his hand as Father in God of the community, as Jesus was proclaimed to be the Son of God by the voice of the Father. The use of the holy oil carried many meanings. Jesus was *Christos*, the Anointed One, and the anointing of Christians emphasized their union with him and their right to the name Christ-ians. In the Old Testament kings and priests are anointed, and Christians are a royal priesthood. The oil also symbolized the Holy Spirit, since the Messianic anointing of Jesus was not with visible oil but with the inward unction of the Holy Spirit.

In terms of ritual structure, the admission to the catechumenate and the election, or choosing of the candidates as "seekers," are rites of separation, setting the catechumens off from the non-Christian society in which they lived. The catechumenate itself is a transition or liminal state, in which the catechumens are no longer pagans, but are not yet baptized Christians. This liminal state is represented by the fact that they were not allowed to attend the Eucharist, to pray with the faithful, or to exchange the kiss of peace. The sacrament of baptism is the great rite of incorporation. The actions of the bishop when the candidates returned to the assembled congregation are acts incorporating them into the body of the faithful, or, to use a later term, confirming their new status. They immediately exercise this new status by doing precisely the things that had previously been forbidden to them: praying with the faithful, exchanging the peace, and participating in the Eucharist.

The initiation was the action of the entire Christian Church. It was presided over by the bishop. The presbyters and deacons had important roles in the actual washing and anointing, and the entire congregation joined in celebrating the Easter Eucharist, the first communion of the newly baptized, with them. Some early documents mention the importance of deaconesses at the baptism of women. The deaconesses went down into the water with the women and anointed their bodies with the holy oil.[53]

The meaning of the action must have been perfectly clear to all who participated. Men, women, and children who had previouly been outside of it were brought into the Christian family. No longer a collection of unrelated individuals, they were now God's people. They underwent a ritual death and resurrection with Christ, and the Holy Spirit came to dwell in them, as he descended upon Jesus at his baptism. By this action they were made new; their past lives, including their sins, were washed away as they became new children of God.

As Christ was anointed with Holy Spirit at his baptism, so they were anointed with the chrism as Christ-ians, as priests and kings to God, and signed with the cross, Christ's own mark. Then as members of the royal and priestly people, the mystical body of Christ, they joined in the Eucharist and received his sacramental body. For them, and for the entire body of Christians, this was the Easter experience. Year by year as Christians were initiated they renewed their own participation in the Paschal mystery, which was their birth into eternal life.

The account in *Apostolic Tradition* ends with the simple statement that the bishop is to tell them privately after the baptism whatever else it is necessary for the new Christians to know. By the fourth century this had become a series of formal lectures on the meaning of the sacraments, *mystagogia*, given by the bishop during Easter Week to the newly baptized and any other Christians who wished to attend. The instructions were regularly given at a daily celebration of the Eucharist attended by the neophytes in their white baptismal robes. The English name Whitsunday is derived indirectly from this practice, since in the colder climate of Britain it was customary to postpone the annual baptism until Pentecost in the hope of warmer weather, and it was then that the newly baptized were present in their white baptismal robes.

The ritual pattern established here continued into the Middle Ages. We find it still being celebrated in Rome at 800 A.D., although by then all of the candidates were infants. Officially today the Church does much the same thing, but the clarity of the ritual pattern has been blurred if not destroyed, and it is no longer clear to most people what we are doing in baptism, confirmation, and first communion, or why we do it.

NOTES

1. Acts 10:38-43 RSV.
2. Philippians 2:11.
3. I Corinthians 11:26.
4. Gregory Dix, *Jew and Greek* (Westminster: Dacre Press, 1953), pp. 102f.

4a. Cf. above, p. 36.

4b. Hebrews 10 and *passim*.

5. *Didache* 9-10, tr. Cyril C. Richardson, *Early Christian Fathers*, Library of Christian Classics 1 (Philadelphia: Westminster, 1953), pp. 175f. (slightly altered).

6. Cf. Louis Finkelstein, "Birkat Ha-Mazon," pp. 213-219; K. Kohler, *Jewish Encyclopedia* 4, art, "Didache" p. 587.

7. Felix L. Cirlot, *The Early Eucharist* (London: S.P.C.K., 1939), pp. 171-175.

8. I Corinthians 16:21; Revelation 22:20.

9. Marianne Micks, *The Future Present* (New York: Seabury, 1970), p. 17.

10. *Ibid.*, p. 15.

11. Gregory Dix, *The Shape of the Liturgy* (Westminster: Dacre Press, 1945), p. 48.

12. Justin, *First Apology* 67, tr. Edward R. Hardy in Richardson, *Fathers*, p. 287.

13. I Corinthians 11:20-22 RSV.

14. Pliny, *Epistles* x. 96, tr. J. Stevenson, *A New Eusebius* (London: S.P.C.K., 1968), p. 14.

15. Tertullian, *Apology* 319; Clement of Alexandria, *Paedogogus* ii. 4-7.

16. Dix, *Shape*, p. 100.

17. Justin, *Apology* 65, ed. Richardson, *Fathers*, pp. 285ff.

18. *Apostolic Tradition* 4, ed. Bernard Botte, *La Tradition Apostolique de Saint Hippolyte*, Liturgiewissenschaftliche Queelen und Forschungen 39 (Münster: Aschendorffsche Verlagsbuchhandlung, 1963), p. 10.

19. Justin, *Apology* 65, pp. 285ff.

20. *Apostolic Tradition* 4.

21. *Tradition* 9, ed. Botte, p. 28 (tr. LLM).

22. My view of *Apostolic Tradition* is given at length in *Baptismal Anointing* (London: S.P.C.K., 1966), Ch. 1.

23. *Worship Supplement* Authorized by the Commission on Worship, The Lutheran Church-Missouri Synod (St. Louis: Concordia, 1969), p. 46.

24. *Sacramentary* (Ottawa; Canadian Catholic Conference, 1974), pp. 597-602. (The Text is identical but the page reference different in other edictions.)

25. *The Draft Proposed Book of Common Prayer* (New York: Church Hymnal Corp., 1976), pp. 369-371.

26. *Tradition* 4, ed. Botte, pp. 10-17 (tr. LLM).

27. Isaiah 6:3.

28. F. E. Brightman, *Liturgies Eastern and Western* 1 (Oxford: Oxford University Press, 1896, 1967), p. 329 (tr. LLM).

29. Justin, *Apology* 66, tr. Richardson, *Fathers*, p. 286.

30. *Didache* 7, tr. Richardson, *Fathers*, p. 174.

31. Justin, *Apology* 61, ed. Richardson, *Fathers*, p. 282.

32. *Tradition* 17, ed. Botte, p. 39.

33. A one-volume collection of English translations of these addresses is Edward Yarnhold, S.J., *The Awe-Inspiring Rites of Initiation* (Slough, England: St. Paul Publications, 1971).

34. Romans 6:3-11 RSV.

35. Eliade, *Rites*, p. x.

36. Galatians 2:20.

37. I Peter 2:9-10 RSV.

38. F. L. Cross, *I Peter, A Paschal Liturgy* (London: Mowbray, 1954).

39. See above, Chapter 1, p. 8.

40. Mark 1:10-11 RSV.

41. *Tradition* 15.

42. Cf. Gavin, *Jewish Antecedents*, p. 33.

43. *Tradition* 17.

44. *Ibid.*, 21.

45. *Ibid.*, 18.

46. *Ibid.*, 20.

47. John Wilkinson, *Egeria's Travels* (London: S.P.C.K. 1971), 45.1, pp. 143f.

48. *Tradition* 35, ed. Botte, p. 82.

49. *Ibid.*, 20.

50. *Egeria* 29-40, pp. 131-140.

51. Augustine, *Confessions* 8.2.

52. *Tradition* 21, ed. Botte, pp. 44-59.

53. E.g. *Didascalia Apostolorum* 16.

4

The Rituals of Christendom

It is not the purpose of this book to treat the history of the Christian liturgy, but it is impossible to move directly from the rituals of the early Church to those of the twentieth century. While in one sense we can say that the rites simply continued to be celebrated, with some revision at the Reformation, until the present, any such statement would be profoundly misleading. If the rites themselves remained substantially intact, the understanding of them changed radically. It has only been in the twentieth century that a revival in many places of the liturgical piety of the first Christian centuries has made the rites of the early Church seem familiar to us.

Liturgical Piety

The history of the worship of the Christian Church is only partially a history of its official forms of worship. It involves also the various social, cultural, and spiritual factors that determine the way the rituals are experienced by the people. The same rites conducted by a tiny, illegal gathering of devoted Christians and by a large congregation gathered in an imperial basilica will almost necessarily produce different psychological effects on the participants. In the words of the Orthodox theologian Alexander Schmemann:

> Above all it is important for the historian of worship to know that the "liturgical piety" of an epoch can in various ways fail to correspond to the liturgy or cult of which this piety is nevertheless the psychological perception or experience. This means that piety can accept the cult in a "key" other than that in which it was conceived and expressed as a text, ceremony, or "rite." Liturgical piety has the strange power of "transposing" texts or ceremonies, of attaching a meaning to them which is not their plain or original meaning. . . . Conservatism and love of the traditional forms of cult plus an extraordinary flexibility in their interpretation; the ability to accept and experience these forms in new ways and to "project" them into psychological and religious experiences stemming often from completely alien sources—such are the characteristics of liturgical piety.[1]

We have already discussed the relationship of the early Church to the Jewish and Hellenistic mystery piety, and the radically new understanding that their belief in the resurrection of Christ gave to the Jewish ritual forms that Christianity continued to use. In the fourth century, with the conversion of Constantine and the transformation of the Church from an illegal to an imperial cult, profound changes in Christian life and self-understanding took place. Not only were the legal sanctions against Christianity removed, but it became socially and politically advantageous to become a Christian. The result was a tremendous increase in the number of catechumens, many of whom brought with them essentially non-Christian understandings of the meaning of the universe, and of life within it. The history of medieval Europe is filled with evidence that although they abandoned the worship of the pagan gods, they did not necessarily abandon their pagan attitudes toward life, or toward religion.

A second important change was that the Christian Church became the public state religion. When Constantine founded his new imperial capital at Constantinople, he built the great Church of the Holy Wisdom, Hagia Sophia, in the center of the city, a location corresponding to that of the Temple of Jupiter Capitolinus in Rome, or the Parthenon in Athens. The Christian bishop was now expected to "offer sacrifice" for the success of the imperial legions, and the Eucharist replaced the great public sacrifices in the life of the state.

The effects of all this upon the Church were all-encompassing and well beyond the scope of our discussion. Let us confine ourselves to some examples of their direct effort on worship. Constantine's greatest personal contribution was unquestionably the building of churches for Christian worship. The *basilica*, the imperial hall in which the Roman magistrate conducted his official business and other civic affairs took place, was the model. The *cathedra*, the bishop's throne, took the place of the magistrate's chair. Constantine also extended to bishops the right to hear certain civil cases at law. Within a century the bishops began to wear the insignia of magistrates, and the ceremonial of the imperial court began to find its way into the Church.

In addition to cathedrals in the cities, Constantine built *martyria*, shrines of witness, where the Church assembled on the site of the death of the martyrs to celebrate their heavenly birthdays. The greatest of these was the Martyrium on the site of the crucifixion in Jerusalem, the present Church of the Holy Sepulchre. Constantine did not invent the cult of the martyrs. It already existed in the second century, but his building of *martyria* tended to increase interest in the cult and to turn its focus from the celebration of the triumph of Christ in his death and rising again as reflected in the deaths of the martyrs to historical commemoration of the saints. The *martyria* became places of pilgrimage, and the relics of the saints were frequently moved to *martyria* built in other places. Constantine's plans for the Church of the Holy Apostles in Constantinople included twelve sarcophagi for the relics of the apostles, with his own tomb in their midst.[2]

What we find developing is an interest in historical commemoration, rather than eschatological hope. It is probably not true that the Church before Constantine had no interest in history,[3] but it is certainly true that the Church of the Christian empire became extremely interested in historical commemorations and sites. The church building of the pre-Constantinian period was called *domus ecclesiae*, the house of the church. Christians specifically rejected the idea that their churches were temples, like the pagan temples or even like the Temple in Jerusalem, that is houses of God.[4] For this reason the Constantinian architects did not attempt to adapt the pagan temple architecture to the Christian churches. For Christians, every place was holy, the true temple of God was in men, not in sacred buildings.

This too began to change. The church became a sanctuary. The Holy Table on which the gifts of the Eucharist were placed became identified with the tomb of the martyr. The church building became the house of

God and his saints. Christianity began to consecrate "holy places."[5] Again the rituals have been "transposed" by the setting against which they are placed.

The sheer increase in size of the Church produced another change which is of long-range importance. It became impossible for the congregation to gather in one place around their bishop. *Apostolic Tradition* sees the Eucharist, at least upon important occasions such as ordinations and baptisms, as celebrated by the bishop surrounded by his presbyters and assisted by his deacons.[6] The liturgy was a paradigm of the structure of the Church as described in the epistles of St. Ignatius of Antioch:

> Be careful, then, to observe a single Eucharist. For there is one flesh of our Lord Jesus Christ, and one cup of his blood that makes us one, and one altar, just as there is one bishop along with the presbytery and the deacons.[7]

Increasingly with the growth of the Church this unity was no longer seen in practice. The bishop ceased to be the "parish priest" of the congregation, and presbyters became the normal celebrants first of the Eucharist, then later of the rites of initiation. The unity of the people around their bishop, which was so obvious to Ignatius in the second century, became increasingly a theoretical and theological conception. The one Eucharist and the one altar gave way to many masses at many altars, to accommodate the needs of increasing numbers of Christians. At first the altars were geographically separated as many parishes of a single diocese. Later they became many altars and many masses in a single church building, as even the theory of the one Eucharist with the Christian people gathered around their bishop with his presbyters receded from understanding.

In the case of baptism, the attempt of the Roman bishops to retain their traditional role in its ministration resulted in the dismemberment of the rite.[8] The laying on of hands and signing with the cross were separated from the rest of the initiation rite to become a separate sacrament of confirmation, administered by the bishop when (frequently, and if) he was available for the purpose. In the Eastern and Gallican rites, in which no separate confirmation developed, the presbyter, the new parish priest, became the normal celebrant of the entire rite of initiation.

Differentiation of Rites

Just as the Roman Empire became too large and too diverse for a single emperor to hold it together, the Christian Church drifted into a parallel separation. The Latin West, the Greek East, and the Syriac Orient, speaking different languages, and not bound together by a common political framework, became increasingly dissimilar. Theological differences that found expression in the classical Christological controversies of the fourth and fifth centuries were reinforced by differences of language and culture. In the Roman West and the Byzantine East Church and empire were one. In those lands that fell under Moslem domination with the rise of Islam in the seventh century, and in those countries even farther east where Syriac-speaking missionaries had brought the Christian gospel, the Church survived in tiny ghettos, drawing in upon themselves in order to preserve their lives and their identities.

The liturgical rites of the early Church became increasingly intertwined with local customs and ethnic traditions, developing along increasingly divergent lines. One example may prove sufficient to illustrate the point. Christians in the West, in the restored Roman Empire of Charlemagne, felt it only proper to accord to the altar as the throne of God the external reverence they offered to the Christian emperor, and so customs such as kneeling for communion and bowing before the altar arose. Among Eastern Christians living under a Moslem caliph, court ceremonial did not have the same appeal, and it became a matter of pride that while they were compelled to grovel in the dust before the heathen caliph, in the church they were able to stand on their feet as free men before their God.

In the West the so-called "fall of Rome" and the barbarian invasions radically changed the situation, and drove a further wedge between Roman and Byzantine ritual developments. The barbarians eventually accepted both Christianity and Roman culture, with which it was to a large extent identified, just as in the nineteenth century missionaries were often identified with the Western colonial powers, so that accepting Christianity became one aspect of accepting "Western culture." The barbarians whom Rome christianized did not always (or even often) understand either Christianity or Roman culture. The old method of individual conversion followed by an extensive catechumenate was abandoned, and whole tribes were frequently baptized *en masse*, following the conversion of their chief.

The Goths, the Franks, the Germans, did not understand Latin, but their own languages were often too crude to use for Christian worship. Frequently they had never been reduced to writing, and Latin was a part of the Roman culture to which the barbarians were being assimilated. If they did not understand the words of the Latin liturgy, they reverenced its sacredness. Inevitably though, it became less and less a communal action and more and more a sacred pageant. The congregation became less participants and more reverent, worshipful spectators. The meaning of the words became lost, eventually even to the majority of the priests, and the meaning of the actions was thereby obscured. A new "mystery" arose in Christian worship in which the rites had themselves become mysterious. New "mystical" interpretations were given to the ceremonies of the mass, which interpreted it as a "passion play," a dramatic reenactment of the life and death of Christ.

In the Byzantine East the Christian empire survived into the fifteenth century. In the great churches of Constantinople the liturgy was accompanied by the offering of the finest in art and music to the glory of God. But here too "mystical" reinterpretation replaced understanding. If the words of the liturgy were still understood, the people were cut off from sight and the Holy Mysteries came to be performed behind a veil, amidst rising clouds of incense. It was no longer the eucharistic prayer of the priest but the many litanies of the deacon to which the congregation responded. As the deacon led the people in prayers of intercession, the priest behind the veil recited silently ("mystically" it came to be called) the ancient prayers of the liturgy. Here too the communal action is obscured.

In both East and West this mysterious numinous quality became characteristic of worship. The church building became a sacrament of heaven, and for those with literally no other contact with either music or art it was indeed a piece of heaven in their midst. The celebration of the liturgy is seen as a time taken out of this life to be with God. Worship removes men from the troubles and cares of the present life to spend an hour with saints and angels in eternity. These ideas were not totally new. The earliest Christians viewed their worship as radically eschatological, but the emphasis began to shift from the expectation that Christ would radically transform the world by his Second Coming and the end of the present age, to the hope that He would save the faithful Christian from the evils of this present life, and bring him to the joys of the heavenly city. This is, of course, at its best a vision that sustains hope and even life in the midst of despair, but it tends to produce indifference to the present state of affairs. At its worst it is "pie in the sky by and by."

The Latin Middle Ages

Probably the greatest change brought by the Middle Ages to the Latin liturgy of the West was the dissolution of the liturgical community. By about the year 1000 it had become customary for the priest to celebrate the mass with his back to the congregation.[9] The mass was considered something the priest did, and the congregation watched, an idea that has by no means disappeared from the present understanding of the Eucharist.

The "private mass" developed first of all in monasteries, and spread from them to the parish churches. Here there was no attempt to continue the liturgical roles: deacon, reader, singer. There was no dialogue with the worshiping community. The priest simply recited the entire text of the rite himself. There was, in fact, no visible worshiping community. At most a single

server might respond to the dialogue originally addressed to the entire community; often there was not
even a token congregation present.

At first, the private mass evolved to meet the peculiar situation of monasteries where there were many
more priests than were needed to preside at the celebrations of the people. What developed was the "low
mass" said by a priest with his back to the people, who
neither heard nor understood what he said. Music,
when it survived, was not sung by the congregation but
performed by a *schola cantorum*, a professional choir.
Often it was not even the chants of the liturgy they
sang, but "religious music" as a background for the
prayers of the people.

The people who were present during the mass were
encouraged to pray their own prayers, and to adore
Christ present in the sacrament. Indeed, religion did
not die. Strong devotion to the person of Christ in his
passion and in the Blessed Sacrament of the Altar became a staple of late medieval piety. The elevation of
the host by the priest, accompanied by the ringing of
bells, became the focus of popular devotion, and the
mass was often thought of as the ritual necessary to
produce the Real Presence of Christ in the sacrament,
so that His people might adore Him.[10]

It has been not unreasonably suggested that this is
not too different from a Quaker meeting. There
everyone sits in silence and waits for the Spirit to speak
to the gathered church. Here the priest, and possibly a
server, perform the ritual. Everyone else kneels or sits
and says his own prayers, listens to the music if there is
any, or even sleeps. Frequently the Holy Spirit speaks
to people in both situations, but not really *through* the
words and actions of the liturgy. Except for the few

moments when the bell is rung at the elevation, both Catholic and Quaker are left alone with God. The Reformation, Counter-Reformation, and Liturgical Movement have somewhat changed this situation for both Protestants and Catholics, but the idea of being alone with God and offering private prayers during the liturgy is still a part of most Western Christians' liturgical piety.

Reception of Communion

In the early Church Christians who were not undergoing ecclesiastical discipline normally received communion whenever they participated in the celebration of the Eucharist. Pagans and catechumens were forbidden to attend the eucharistic celebration. Catechumens were regularly dismissed with a prayer and blessing following the Scripture readings and sermon. In some places penitents, baptized Christians who were forbidden to participate in the Eucharist for a period as part of a ritual process of reconciliation to the Church after confessing serious sin, were permitted to remain kneeling in the church building during the celebration. But Christians in good standing participated both by offering their gifts at the offertory, and by receiving communion.

After the conversion of Constantine the practice of Christians' attending the Eucharist but not receiving communion began to grow. Probably preachers had so heavily emphasized the dangers of unworthy participation that even the faithful began to be reluctant to receive. The "worldly" life of Christians in the days after the end of the persecutions seemed to many a sharp contrast to the ascetic lives of the monks and hermits, and the devotion of the martyrs and confessors of the earlier period. More and more lay people came to receive the sacrament only after extensive preparation. Eventually the custom became for most people to receive only at Easter, after a Lent of penitential preparation.

By the sixteenth century annual communion at Easter had become the normal practice of the Western Church. This had further changed the focus of liturgical piety. As long as regular participation by the laity in the act of communion was general, it was the natural climax of the rite. The congregation by receiving the Body and Blood of Christ participated in the eucharistic sacrifice and its benefits. With the decline of communion, the elevation of the host became the focus of adoration, and new theological concepts of how lay people participated in the "fruits" of the mass began to develop.[11]

All of the major Reformers, with the exception of Zwingli, wished the Eucharist with the general communion of the faithful to be the normal Sunday service of the Church. They correctly saw in noncommunicating attendance the source of what they believed to be false teachings about the "sacrifice of the mass." The tradition of popular piety was too strong for them, however, and they uniformly failed to introduce weekly communion. They succeeded instead in ending the weekly celebration of the Eucharist, so that monthly or even quarterly communion became customary. One of the "demands" made by the conservatives who rioted against the introduction of the First Prayer Book in 1549 was that they should be required to receive communion only at Easter.[12]

Among Roman Catholics regular weekly communion did not become usual until the reforms of Pius X in the first decade of the twentieth century.[13] Non-communicating attendance at mass remained the norm until then.

It would be difficult to underestimate the profound effect on the understanding of the Eucharist which resulted from its separation in the popular mind from the receiving of communion among Catholics, and its displacement as the normal Sunday service and relegation to the status of an occasional "communion service" among Protestants. For both, the reception of communion became a sort of pious "extra" rather than integral to the core of regular Sunday worship.

The Effect of the Reformation

The "attack on the mass" that was a part of the Reformation protest was not an attack upon the celebration of the Eucharist per se. The authority of the synoptic gospels and St. Paul assured the celebration of the Lord's Supper a place in the worship of the Reformers. Luther, Calvin, and the Anglican Reformers all considered the celebration of the Supper to be the proper Christian service for the Lord's Day. Their concern was with what they considered to be serious abuses that separated the practice of the Catholic Church from that of the New Testament. Even Zwingli's drastic reform which called for the celebration of the Lord's Supper only four times a year considered itself to have "reclaimed the Supper and re-established it in its proper use."[14]

It was the universal desire of the Reformers to reestablish worship in conformity with the New Testament Church, yet the materials that would have been necessary to attempt any such restoration were lacking to them. They knew little or nothing of the worship of the early Church. The Latin liturgy of the Middle Ages was the sole form of worship known to them. Archbishop Cranmer was apparently familiar with the Greek liturgy that had been published in Latin translation in 1528, from which he took "a Prayer of Chrysostome," and with some Medieval Spanish rites, but the liturgies of the early Church were totally unknown. It was therefore impossible for them to do what they wished to do on any scientific basis. Often serious historical errors were made in the attempt to restore a purer earlier usage.

One principle the Reformers put into practice was that worship should be in a language people could understand, and almost invariably the first reformed liturgy of a place was a "purified" translation of the Latin mass into the local vernacular. The Prayer Book of 1549 and the *Deutsche Messe* of Luther are outstanding examples. Sometimes the second wave of reform attempted to abolish "ritual worship" altogether, and simple services based on New Testament models took the place of the traditional liturgy. Generally Anglicans and Lutherans retained revised forms of the traditional rituals, while Calvinists abandoned much of the traditional structure in favor of a simpler service of Word and Sacrament.

We have already mentioned the renewed focus on communion that was characteristic of the vernacular liturgies and its undesired result, the relegation of the Eucharist to the place of an occasional service, while a liturgy of the Word alone became the normal Sunday service. It was probably inevitable that the neglect of the Word in the Middle Ages should have produced a neglect of ritual action as a reaction. Louis Bouyer has written well:

> If words and rites are distinct and are to a certain extent opposed, their constant connection must mean a natural relationship. This is so true that a decisive dominance of one over the other effects a change in the dominant element itself which seems to foretell the downfall of religion and perhaps quite simply of the religious man himself. . . .
>
> If the word becomes obscured the rite itself will disintegrate.[15]

If Medieval worship was characterized by the complete domination of word by rite, post-Reformation worship has tended to reduce ritual to a collection of audiovisual aids to make the meaning of the spoken word clearer. Even modern Roman Catholic worship tends toward a certain embarrassment with its ritual and toward the overwhelming of the action with verbal explanations. In the so-called "nonliturgical" churches ritual was as completely eliminated as possible. Zwingli had written:

> No doubt, all believers are well aware of how much damage and apostasy from God have resulted heretofore from the great mass of ceremonies. We therefore think it best to prescribe as little ceremonial and churchly custom as we can for our people's use of this Supper—which is also a ceremony, but instituted by Christ—lest we yield again, in time, to the old error.[16]

The warning of Zwingli was taken to heart and in many churches worship was reduced to hearing the Word read and preached, together with prayer by the minister. Even in the Anglican and Lutheran traditions, which retained the traditional ritual structures, this frame of mind, a sort of nonliturgical piety, profoundly influenced the people's understanding of their liturgy, which was often seen as simply an appropriate "setting" for the preaching of the Word.

The Reformation did, nevertheless, produce vernacular liturgies in which lay people can and do participate actively. The Roman Catholic anthropologist Mary Douglas has commented,

> Between Catholic and Anglican celebrations of the Eucharist there is a shift from the emphasis on ritual efficacy in the first to the emphasis on a commemorative rite in the second.[17]

What she is describing, however, is not really a difference between churches but the tendency toward the privatizing of religious experience and contempt for external forms that she finds characteristic of English and American (as opposed to Irish) Roman Catholicism as well. It is certainly true that Anglicans, Lutherans, and Roman Catholics all tend to look at the rituals in which they participate from slightly different points of view, but it is hard to explain these differences accurately and it is probably impossible to draw lines between the churches, rather than between two tendencies found in Western Christianity since the Middle Ages and the Reformation.

From the Roman Catholic point of view, the principal effect of the adoption of vernacular worship by the Reformation was to rigidify and fossilize Roman

Catholic opposition to change. So suspicious of every suggestion of reform did the ecclesiastical authorities become that the mass in 1950 was substantially the same as the mass in 1550. The normal processes of ritual development and liturgical change were artificially halted until the *aggiornamento* of Pope John XXIII plunged his church into making four centuries worth of accumulated changes in a decade.

Among Anglicans a new form of liturgical piety developed in which the Prayer Book itself became the focus of religion, and active participation in the rites (which normally meant vocal participation) became the mark of piety. The use of a particular ritual was seen as the differentia of Anglicanism from other churches and loyalty to the Book of Common Prayer became identified with loyalty to the church. Usually this is interpreted as loyalty to the words, not to the ritual actions of the Prayer Book.

The End of Christendom

The liturgical era upon which we have been reflecting in this chapter is that of Christendom, in which Christianity and the state are seen as either identical or closely allied. Today it is widely recognized that Christendom has broken down, and that Christianity finds itself in a new situation over against the secular state. This is the present situation with which we shall concern ourselves in the next chapter.

NOTES

1. Alexander Schmemann, *Introduction to Liturgical Theology*, Library of Orthodox Theology 4 (Portland, Me.:

American Orthodox Press, 1966), p. 77.

2. Massey H. Shepherd, "Liturgical Expressions of the Constantinian Triumph," *Dumbarton Oaks Papers* 21 (Washington: Dumbarton Oaks Center for Byzantine Studies, 1967), p. 75.

3. Cf. Thomas J. Talley, "History and Eschatology in the Primitive Pascha," *Worship* 47 (1973), pp. 212-221.

4. Shepherd, "Expressions," pp. 70-75.

5. Schmemann, *Introduction*, pp. 89-92.

6. *Apostolic Tradition* 4, 21, ed. Botte, pp. 10, 54.

7. Ignatius, *Philadelphians* 4, tr. Richardson, *Fathers*, p. 108.

8. Cf. J.D.C. Fisher, *Christian Initiation: Baptism in the Medieval West*, Alcuin Club Collections 47 (London: SPCK, 1965); Mitchell, *Anointing*, Ch. 5, pp. 80-171.

9. Theodor Klauser, *A Short History of the Western Liturgy* (London: Oxford University Press, 1969), p. 101.

10. John J. Hughes, *Stewards of the Lord* (London: Sheed and Ward, 1970), pp. 81, 83.

11. *Ibid.*, pp. 52ff.

12. Francis Procter and Walter H. Frere, *A New History of the Book of Common Prayer* (London: Macmillan, 1958), p. 57.

13. Klauser, *History*, p. 121.

14. Ulrich Zwingli, *Action or Use of the Lord's Supper*, 1525, tr. Bard Thompson, *Liturgies of the Western Church* (Cleveland: Meredian Books, 1961), p. 149.

15. Bouyer, *Rite*, pp. 55, 57.

16. Zwingli, *Action*, tr. Thompson, *Liturgies*, p. 149.

17. Mary Douglas, *Natural Symbols: Explorations in Cosmology* (New York: Random House, 1972), p. 27.

5

Ritual Today

Any attempt to deal with the contemporary situation necessarily involves a lack of historical perspective. At the same time it makes possible a knowledge of the subject "from within" that historical discussion lacks. There is, of course, a wide spectrum of literature available on the contemporary world, and the place of ritual within it, from sociological studies to religious tracts.[1] In the last chapter the work of Mary Douglas, *Natural Symbols*, was cited, more or less in passing. Let us begin with a more extensive citation:

> One of the gravest problems of our day is the lack of commitment to common symbols. . . . But more mysterious is a wide-spread explicit rejection of rituals as such. Ritual has become a bad word signifying empty conformity. We are witnessing a revolt against formalism, even against form.[2]

She describes this revolt as having three phases:

> First, there is the contempt of external ritual forms; second, there is a private internalizing of religious experience; third there is the move to humanist philanthropy. When the third stage is under way, the symbolic life of the spirit is finished.[3]

In her own Roman Catholic Church, she finds this movement well under way and exemplified by the divergent attitudes of the British hierarchy and the "Bog Irish" unskilled workmen of England toward Friday abstinence. For the bishops, the failure of Friday abstinence to point to the crucifixion of Christ meant that it was no longer meaningful and should be abandoned. On the other hand, Douglas writes,

> Symbols which are tenaciously adhered to can hardly be dismisssd as altogether meaningless. They must mean something. . . . This is what the rule of Friday abstinence can signify. No empty symbol, it means allegiance to a humble home in Ireland and to a glorious tradition in Rome. These allegiances are something to be proud of in the humiliation of the unskilled labourer's lot.[4]

By contrast, she finds a very different view of ritual expressed by her clerical friends:

> I am told that ritual conformity is not a valid form of personal commitment and is not compatible with the full development of the personality; also that the replacement of ritual conformity with rational commitment will give greater meaning to the lives of Christians. Furthermore if Christianity is to be saved for future generations, ritualism must be rooted out, as if it were a weed choking the life of the spirit.[5]

I am probably more comfortable with Professor Douglas' clerical friends than with her "Bog Irish" relatives, but she raises two important points about religious ritual in contemporary life. The first is that its practitioners, the clergy, are often ill at ease with it; and the second is that even when it has ceased to serve its original purpose, it may acquire a new one for many people. The history of religious ritual provides many examples of the development of new meanings for rites that had lost their original sense. We seem always more ready to reinterpret a ritual than to abandon it.

One function of ritual in the present world is to give a sense of identity and community to those who would otherwise have none. The obvious parallel between the Friday abstinence of the "Bog Irish" and the abstinence from pork practiced by many otherwise nonreligious Jews should convince us of the importance of symbolic actions in establishing ethnic identity. The Jews of the diaspora and the Irish immigrants to England and North America are only the most obvious examples of the alienation and rootlessness that are almost endemic in the world today. The "ethnic" who celebrates with old country folk dancing, the Scottish-American who wears a kilt and plays the bagpipe, the black who eats "soul food" and wears an Afro, and the Southerner who waves the Confederate battle flag and sings Dixie are ritualizing, and thereby making real to themselves who they are and where they come from.

In nothing, perhaps, is this ritual sense of identity so marked as in the passion with which many Americans defend beginning the school day with prayer, or the common recitation of the Pledge of Allegiance to the Flag. Opposition to these civic rites is "un-American" in much the same sense as the refusal of the early Christians to burn incense to Caesar must have been considered "un-Roman."

Secular Rituals

If Americans are ill at ease with ritual in church, they use it freely in many other aspects of their life. The popularity of the ritualism of fraternal orders among those who oppose any form of ecclesiastical ceremonial is too well known to require further elaboration. We may laugh at the ritual of the Miss America pageant, or of the Academy Awards presentation, but they are watched by millions of people. "Here she comes, Miss America," and "The envelope, please!" are ritual formulae known to all.

Every fall at the University of Notre Dame I participate in a number of extremely formal rituals. They are not held in the University Church of the Sacred Heart, but in the football stadium. I do not refer to the game itself, although the ritual nature of games is a significant study.[6] I refer to the activities that precede and follow the game.

First an announcement is made of the "band of the Fighting Irish," and, preceded by the kilted Irish Guard composed of men at least 6'2" in height, the uniformed band comes onto the field, to the accompaniment of the cheers of 50,000 people. The band, using always the same ritual "high step," marches to midfield, faces the opponents' bench and plays their football song. Then, turning from the region of darkness to the region of light, it leads the assembled congregation in "the greatest of all fight songs, the Notre Dame Victory March." The U.S. flag is then presented to the Irish Guard by appropriate dignitaries, while the band plays America the Beautiful. The audience, now no longer spectators but participants, joins in singing the hymn while the procession moves to the flag pole. If the opponents' band is present, their leader is invited to "concelebrate" by conducting the National Anthem while the flag is raised.

When the game is about to resume after halftime, the students pour out onto the playing field and form two lines through which the team and coaches run, led by the cheer leaders, as they return to the field. Their appearance is preceded by the rhythmic chanting of, "Here come the Irish!" The entire ritual is performed in exactly the same way before every home game.

After the game a shorter ritual is similarly performed. It involves the shouting of the Notre Dame Victory March to accompany a victory dance performed by the kilted Guardsmen. A somewhat different dance step is used upon the few occasions when the opponents win, but the Victory March is still sung as an eschatological act of faith.

Those who have attended football games of other colleges or high schools will doubtless recognize this as similar to rituals they have experienced. I have been accustomed, in teaching at Notre Dame, to use this particular example to point out to students that it is possible to involve large numbers of people intensively in a highly ritualistic activity. I hardly need to point out that this seldom happens in church.

A more serious example of secular ritual is "flag burning." The intense emotions provoked by this particular form of symbolic action give evidence of its power. I am not certain that those who burned the American flag as a symbol of their opposition to the Vietnam War conveyed precisely the meaning they wished, but they certainly did convey a message. The flag that was burned was by no means seen as an "empty symbol." Its burning was considered to be patriotic, or traitorous, but not irrelevant. Serious legislatures enacted statutes providing prison terms for the offenders. Dr. James White, of Southern Methodist University, has aptly commented on the irony by which many of the same people who denounced the "flag-burners" and demanded their arrest spoke of the bread and wine of the Eucharist as "only a symbol!"[7]

Perhaps some of the contemporary impatience with ritual is a justified reaction to the poor quality of much of the ritual in which we are constrained to participate. As an academic, and therefore a professional attender of commencements, my view may be somewhat jaundiced, but I do not believe most people are moved by the rites of high school or college commencements. The "sermons" are often less relevant and less well delivered than those they hear in church, and the ritual conferring of degrees often does not carry conviction. My own college graduation was conducted in Latin, a language the school president himself clearly did not understand. The gowns are usually worn in a way that makes clear that the wearers are not only physically uncomfortable, but spiritually uncomfortable at being so strangely garbed. In short, it is usually only our concern for one or more of the graduates that enables us to endure the ceremony.

The philosopher Josef Pieper has written that it is impossible to create a truly secular festival:

> Secular as well as religious festivals have their roots in the rituals of worship. Otherwise what arises is not a profane festival, but something quite artificial, which is either an embarrassment or . . . a new and more strenuous kind of work.[8]

It is likely that it is precisely the attempt to cut it loose from its religious roots that vitiates so much American secular ritual, and prevents it from achieving what it sets out to accomplish. This, in turn, can create a sense of embarrassment or an expectancy of shallowness that carries over into religious rituals.

Festivity, which for Pieper is rooted and grounded in ritual worship, is made possibly only by the affirmation of the world and man within it. The cynicism and negativism of much of contemporary culture is destructive of joy and festivity, and renders ritual worship itself absurd:

> Whoever refuses assent to reality as a whole, no matter how well off he may be, is by that fact incapacitated for either joy or festivity. Festivity is impossible to the nay-sayer. The more money he has, and above all the more leisure, the more desperate is this impossibility to him.[9]

In the latter part of his book Pieper discusses the pseudo-festivals of the French Revolution and the antifestivals of Nazi Germany and the Communist states. This same theme has been pursued by Ernest Koenker in his *Secular Salvations*,[10] an investigation of what he calls the rites and symbols of political religions. Any discussion of these would take us too far afield, but we need to be aware of them as the rituals of self-consciously anti-Christian religions, intended to embody a new faith in new rites. Koenker makes this especially clear in his discussion of the new rites of passage whih are intended to replace those of the Christian Church, such as Nazi "Life Festivals" or East German Youth Dedications.

Pieper's warning needs to be heard:

> The place in life which should naturally be oc-
> cupied by real festivity cannot remain empty. And
> when real festivals are no longer celebrated, for
> whatever reasons, the susceptibility to artificial
> ones grows.[11]

The same principle may well apply to ritual worship in general. The downgrading of ritual worship in
our society is probably one cause of the proliferation of
secular ritual.

Liturgy and Community

It is almost a commonplace among contemporary
students of Christian liturgy that the liturgical problems of the present do not admit of liturgical solutions,
for they are but symptomatic of a malaise of society.
The community that gathers to celebrate the liturgy is
not a true community but an aggregation of individuals.
The struggle to restore the liturgical community has
been one of the chief concerns of the twentieth-century
Liturgical Movement. Actually, it is not the liturgical
community, but all community which is conspicuously
lacking in modern urban life. As Fr. A. Gabriel Hebert,
one of the pioneers of the Liturgical Movement in the
Church of England, wrote in 1935, "The task of the
Church in the future will be to re-create a social life."[12]
Frederick Nietzsche wrote in the 1870s, "The trick
is not to arrange a festival, but to find people who can
enjoy it."[13] In the same way the agenda for contemporary ritual worship is probably not the celebration of
beautiful services but the development of communities

that will want to celebrate them. For the Christian this is not simply a necessary act of prudence to ensure a congregation for his rites, but a direct corollary of Incarnational religion, of belief in a God who so loved the world that he gave his only Son for its redemption.

This means that the Christian community must be more than a group of like-minded people who are willing to perform certain rituals together. It must be, in traditional language, a cell in the Mystical Body of Christ. These words of a sermon of St. Augustine have commended themselves to teachers of the liturgy:

> If now you have received aright, you are what you have received: and so the Apostle expounds the Sacrament of the Lord's Table: *We who are many are one bread one body.* The bread signifies to you how you ought to love unity. It was made out of many grains of wheat, which were originally separate, but were united by application of water, by a kind of rubbing together and baked with fire. So have you been ground together by the fast and the exorcism, wetted in Baptism, and baked by the fire of Christ and the mystery of the Holy Spirit . . . and you are made bread, which is the Body of Christ: and here is the symbol of unity.[14]

In nothing do the words of Christian liturgy strike the ears of contemporary men and women as "empty ritual" so much as when they speak of a loving, Spirit-filled community where none is visible. Our contemporary parishes, not only large and impersonal ones but also small and cliquy ones, often belie in their actions the words of their worship. This is not a new danger. St. Paul complained of it to the Corinthians. We may, nonetheless, ask what the Church is doing to fight against this evil.

The problem of community in liturgy is seen as more acute today because the rural society with its village church which has formed the staple of Christendom since the fall of the Roman Empire has given way to a mass impersonal urban industrial society in which the average churchgoer never meets his fellow worshipers except in church. He does not bring his community into the church with him. He must find it there. The alternative is individualism and privatized religion, which is not only false to the nature of the liturgy but irrelevant to the needs of our society. Irrelevance is, in fact, precisely the charge most frequently brought against ritual worship today.

The Liturgical Movement

The twin poles of the Liturgical Movement, which is the great fact in the history of Christian worship in the twentieth century, are *liturgy* and *life* and their necessary interrelation. One popular presentation put it this way:

> Every part of our parish life must be related to this fellowship at the Altar where we are all members one of another. Every part of our parish life must be offered here to God for redemption. This is the true meaning of sacrifice.[15]

It is important to begin here, because the primary concern of the Movement has not been with the reform of worship, but with the renewal of the common life in

Christ. It is because that life is expressed and focused in worship that it has concerned itself with the reform and renewal of rites. This is nowhere more clearly expressed than in the opening paragraphs of the Constitution on the Sacred Liturgy of Vatican Council II, which represents the climax of the work of the Liturgical Movement within the Roman Catholic Church.

The Constitution begins by stating the aims of the Council: (1) the strengthening of Christian life, (2) the adaptation to contemporary needs of those institutions subject to chage, (3) the promotion of unity among Christians, and (4) the conversion of the world. It seeks to accomplish these goals first of all by the reform and promotion of the liturgy:

> For the liturgy . . . is the outstanding means whereby the faithful may express in their lives, and manifest to others, the mystery of Christ and the real nature of the true Church.[16]

The Liturgical Movement, then, is a primary aspect of the attempt of the Christian Church to address itself to the world of today. It seeks to bring the Light of the Gospel to bear on the everyday lives of ordinary Christians, creating in the Church a community that can offer its life to God in Christ and then carry it out to affect the life of the world. It sees the way to do this in the revitalization and reform of the historic ritual worship of Christians. Of course, not everyone, nor even every Christian, believes this is possible. Romano Guardini, a distinguished European liturgical scholar, addressed a provocative open letter to a liturgical conference in 1964 in which he asked if it would not be more honest to give up the traditional liturgical act completely and make a fresh start.[17] Guardini himself apparently did not think so, but he recognized that many people did.

It is not only those who think that ritual worship has no place in contemporary life who oppose its reform and renewal. There are others who find in the archaism of liturgical forms a retreat from an uncongenial present. They wish the Church to provide a return to a past "age of faith," either with the Gothic architecture and Gregorian chant of the Middle Ages, or the "simple religion" of the New Testament.

The nineteenth-century Liturgical Movement associated with the Benedictine Abbey of Solesmes and the work of Dom Prosper Guéranger was really a part of the more general Romantic movement.[18] It sought to bridge the gap between the Latin liturgy and modern man by changing modern man, and to the extent that it was successful, it succeeded by recreating the life of the Middle Ages at Solesmes. It was, however, not a creation but a copy. It took people out of their own culture and formed a liturgical subculture for whom alone the ritual was relevant.

Our most obvious legacy of this movement, and a testimony to its importance, are the countless medieval churches built by Christians of all denominations throughout the United States. Some, like the National Cathedral of St. Peter and St. Paul in Washington, are buildings of great beauty. Others are incomparably ugly, breathing the spirit of neither the Middle Ages nor the present. All raise serious questions about the contemporaneity of the religion of which they are the symbols. Old buildings speak of an ongoing tradition. New "old buildings" give a more uncertain message.

The most important effects of the movement were

the scholarly work done in the recovery of Gregorian Chant and the impetus given to the historical study of the rites themselves. This scholarship has resulted not only in the recovery and editing of many early texts that increase our store of information about liturgical history, but it has enabled us to understand the structure and dynamics of the liturgy in a way that was impossible, for example, in the sixteenth century. This scholarship was one of the forces that made possible the Liturgical Movement of the present century. In the words of a recent commentator:

> The paradox of Guéranger's career is that within what was universally understood to be a reactionary movement at his death were elements which evolved into the expression of Christianity most suited to industrial conditions.[19]

Louis Bouyer considers the address of Dom Lambert Beauduin at a Catholic Conference at Malines in Belgium in 1909 to be the "moment" that marks the beginning of the contemporary Liturgical Movement.[20]

> The liturgy itself [properly] understood is meant to be the well-spring of spiritual vitality and to provide the framework for Christian living, not only for individuals, not only for some Christians, but for the whole Christian people in the Church.[21]

It is not necessary for us to give a history of the Liturgical Movement, and its spread from the Roman Catholic Church in Belgium and Germany throughout the world and across ecclesiastical borders into Anglican, Lutheran, and Reformed Churches.[22] We must, nevertheless, mention again the work of Dom Odo Casel, whose work on pagan and Christian mysteries was quoted in chapter two. Casel was unquestionably the great theologian of the Liturgical Movement, and his mystery-theology was in its main outlines accepted by Vatican Council II and embodied in the teaching of the Sacred Constitution on the Liturgy. Charles Davis clearly summarized this aspect of Casel's teaching in these paragraphs:

> Casel and his followers insist that we are Christians only because there is realized in us what was realized in Christ. The mystery of Christ extends also to us and embraces us, so that we not merely receive grace from the saving work of Christ, but also enter into that work itself. Hence we must make contact, not only with Christ and His grace, but also with the saving acts of Christ.

> We do this in the Liturgy in which the saving acts of Christ are made present sacramentally. This teaching of the theology of the mysteries means that it involves an all-embracing conception of the Christian life itself, and is not simply an interpretation of the liturgy.[23]

This is the theology underlying the words of the Constitution:

> By baptism men are plunged into the paschal mystery of Christ: they die with him, are buried with him, and rise with him: they receive the spirit of adoption as sons "in which we cry: Abba, Father," and thus become the true adorers whom the Father

seeks. In like manner, as often as they eat the supper of the Lord they proclaim the death of the
Lord until he comes. . . .[24]

At the practical level this meant an emphasis on
the baptismal priesthood of the Christian people and
the necessity of their "full, conscious, and active participation in liturgical celebrations."[25] This represents a
move away from the Medieval and Reformation cleri-
calism that afflicted both Catholic and Protestant worship and a return to an earlier understanding of the
meaning of ritual worship. Louis Bouyer entitled the
chapter of his *Liturgical Piety* on the beginnings of the
20th century Liturgical Movement "From the Romantic Reaction to the Patristic Ideal of Liturgy."
Sometimes the point of the Movement was missed
and enthusiasts merely substituted an archeological reconstruction of third century worship for thirteenth, but
at least the principles of the worship of the patristic age
were better and lent themselves more readily to the restoration of liturgical worship to its place as the focus of
life in Christ. One Anglican layman addressed himself
to the problem this way, and in so doing expressed the
best pastoral concerns of the Movement:

There are large numbers of people in our own
Anglican Church (and I am by no means excluding
any one of the four orders: bishops, priests, deacons, and laymen) whose awareness of the Liturgical Movement is so flimsy that they equate a
mere ceremony, such as an offertory procession or
a gospel procession, with the Liturgical Movement
itself. If such ceremonies are introduced into a
parish without a careful, *pastoral* exposition of

their symbolic significance they become mere
forms and are in no sense representative of what
the Liturgical Movement is trying to achieve. . . .

The Liturgical Movement has its roots very deep
in the soil of an *ecclesiology* which conceives of all
members of the Church as having been "called of
Jesus Christ" in their capacity of *peculia* or especial possessions of God (1 Pet. 2:9) to bear witness
to him in whatever nook and cranny of the world
they may happen to find themselves.

It has its roots very deep in the soil of a *sacramental theology* which sees clearly that God mediates
his grace through his creatures—whether animal or
vegetable or mineral. . . .

Finally, and most importantly, the Liturgical
Movement has its roots deep in the soil of *pastoral
theology*, with especial emphasis on the homiletical
and exegetical function of the minister in his
parish. His people, no less than he himself, must
know precisely what it is they are doing, what they
are engaged in, in the Church's greatest act of
worship.[26]

The inevitable result of this concern was a demand
for liturgical reform as the necessary condition of liturgical renewal. Among Roman Catholics the revision of
the liturgical books and the celebration of the sacraments in the vernacular became the focus of attention.
Among Anglicans Prayer Book revision and the use of
contemporary English came to be the dominant concerns. For Lutherans the work of the Inter-Lutheran

Commission on Worship was the most obvious fruit of the movement. In fact, throughout the Christian churches, the revision of service books and a new and deeper appreciation of forms of worship came to the fore. In one respect this emphasis on new forms is unfortunate as it focused attention on liturgical change instead of church renewal. The expression and manifestation of the mystery of Christ obviously cannot be reduced to the revising of the text of a ritual, no matter how sound the principles of that revision. The most liturgical revision can hope to do is to remove distortions and encumbrances so that the celebration of the sacraments can be clear channels of communion with the dying and rising Lord who unites us to himself in ritual acts of baptism and Eucharist.[27]

The Ambiguous Present

We seem to be seeing two contradictory tendencies simultaneously at work in the present. One is that described by Mary Douglas as the movement away from ritualism, which seeks to substitute a private internalizing of religious experience for external ritual actions. She writes:

> The devotion to the sacraments, then, depends on a frame of mind which values external forms and is ready to credit them with special efficacy. . . . Many of the current attempts to reform the Christian liturgy suppose that, as the old symbols have lost their meaning, the problem is to find new symbols or to revivify the meaning of the old ones. This could be a total waste of effort if, as I argue,

people at different historic periods are more or less sensitive to signs as such. Some people are deaf or blind to non-verbal signals. I argue that the perception of symbols in general, as well as their interpretation, is socially determined.[28]

There is certainly a general antisymbolic prejudice or blindness in contemporary American society, but there are also signs of increasing interest in and sensitivity to symbols. Nonverbal communication and "body language," for example, are increasingly appreciated.

Some would argue, of course, that contemporary concern with ritual is only the most recent method of "fiddling while Rome burns." Certainly, the retreat into the sacristy will not meet the needs of the present age, but this is not what the Liturgical Movement has as its goals. I would agree with Mary Douglas that we cannot look at ritual in the same way today as in the past, but this does not mean that we should abandon it.

Marshall McLuhan has suggested that there are good nonreligious reasons why the Liturgical Movement has taken place in the twentieth century. Working from his theories of visual and oral media, he writes:

It might baffle many to explain why there should be such a profound liturgical revival in our time, unless they were aware of the essential oral character of the electric "field." Today there is a "High Church" movement within Presbyterianism as well as in many other sects. The merely individual and visual aspects of worship no longer satisfy. . . . The "simultaneous field" of electric information structures, today reconstitutes the conditions and need for dialogue and participation, rather than specialism and private initiate in all levels of social experience.[29]

These are indeed precisely the concerns of the Liturgical Movement in the celebration of rites. This is certainly a rejection of many of the Medieval and Renaissance values that had become attached to Christian rites. McLuhan associated them with the "print culture" and "visual segmentation."[30] It does indeed represent a return to an earlier understanding of ritual, one that sees worship as an experience, in almost the sense in which Aristotle considered the Eleusinian mysteries to be an experience. Marianne Micks describes Christian worship as "a dance both grave and gay,"[31] and goes on to conclude:

> The symbols of Christian worship cannot be invented; they are given. Contemporary liturgists know well that artificial symbols are not symbols but traps. The work facing Christian worshippers as they respond to the new world is not to contrive a new symbolic language, but to learn with expectation and gladness the full vocabulary of making eucharist.[32]

With this conclusion I would heartily agree. We cannot create new symbols, we must deal with those we have inherited. They are the only ones there are. A new ritual is like a new antique. On the other hand, Paul Tillich has reminded us that though we cannot manufacture new symbols, we can allow old ones to fossilize. A symbolic act will not survive forever of its own momentum. Some ritual acts once charged with meaning no longer mean anything at all except to historians, and attempts to revive them are doomed to failure.

We cannot expect simply to revive the rituals of the early Church, for we do not live in the patristic era any more than we do in the Middle Ages or the nineteenth century. Medieval Christendom adopted, adapted, and thereby profoundly changed the rituals of the early Church which it preserved. We must do the same. The process is similar to that of revising a hymnal. Some tunes are dropped, either because they are bad tunes, or because they are not in harmony with the present age. New tunes are added, some recently composed, but also many older ones which had not previously been included. Some tunes which had been dropped in the previous revision will be restored "by popular demand," or because serious musicians recognize their intrinsic worth.

We are in possession today of more knowledge about the history and inner nature of Christian ritual than at any time in the past. We are better able to distinguish the core of Christian worship from the embellishments added to it by succeeding ages. If we see the fallacy of identifying Christianity with Western culture, we need also to avoid identifying it with Medieval, Byzantine, Elizabethan, or Hellenistic culture. We can choose those developments that will commend Christianity to our own time and place and reject others. Here the Constitution on the Sacred Liturgy strikes a proper balance:

> The liturgy is made up of immutable elements divinely instituted, and of elements subject to change. These not only may but ought to be changed with the passage of time if they have suffered from the intrusion of anything out of har-

mony with the inner nature of the liturgy or have
become unsuited to it.[33]

Not only time but place and culture may require a
different approach, and the Constitution condemns a
"rigid uniformity" and speaks of "legitimate variations
and adaptations to different groups, regions, and peoples."[34] The indigenization of liturgy this envisions has
certain inherent risks. The "translation" may alter the
message the rite communicates. The use of bread and
wine for the Eucharist in a country which grows neither
wheat nor grapes, for example, raises serious problems,
but so does the substitution of rice-cakes and tea. Certainly the rites cannot be cut completely loose from
their historical roots in first-century Palestine, or they
will cease to identify us with the Jesus who was born in
the days of Herod the King. On the other hand, the
Catholic Church has always claimed to be universal, for
all times and all places. It is part of the meaning of
Catholic.

I do not pretend that using the religious rituals we
have inherited from the past is easy for us. I do believe
it is necessary. Our lack of a common symbolic language is, as Mary Douglas has reminded us, a serious
problem; but it is more of a problem when looking at
Friday abstinence than when looking at the central
symbolic actions of Christian ritual. Eating, drinking,
washing, laying on a hand, loving, and sharing are understood. What is not understood, or is rejected, is the
formal use of these symbolic acts without any evidence
of interior commitment by the actors.

Many people would say that actions have to be
spontaneous to be genuine. Fr. Clarence Rivers, a black

Roman Catholic priest, has given the best answer I have heard:

> Don't be fooled. Spontaneity takes a great deal of practice. Spontaneity is an illusion. A great deal of exercise is required before an expression can appear spontaneous. For example, when a youngster is beginning a course in gymnastics, he or she is terribly awkward, but really very spontaneous. A veteran gymnast, on the other hand, appears to be completely spontaneous, and yet his or her appearance of spontaneity is something that has taken years and years of practice.[35]

Ritual acts may be spontaneous, but they are taken from a great tradition of symbolic acts. We understand their meaning, because we are a part of the same tradition.

Josef Pieper, in the work we have already quoted in this chapter, wrote:

> In celebrating festivals festively, man passes beyond the barriers of the present life on earth. . . . Through [festivity] the celebrant becomes aware of, and may enter, the greater reality which gives a wider perspective on the world of everyday work, even as it supports it.[36]

> The ritual festival is the most festive form that festivity can possibly take.[37]

This may seem a strange place for a study of the meaning of ritual to wind up. But ultimately the meaning of ritual is festivity, the celebration of redeemed creation and ourselves as a part of it. It is a participation in the Divine life, and a sharing in its love. For Christians this means union and communion with Jesus Christ in the paschal mystery of his death and rising again, with its promise of abundant life and fulness of joy. If ritual worship offers us less than that, we have been cheated.

NOTES

1. A list of such books would inevitably be seriously incomplete. One important book which addresses itself to the problem of contemporary worship from a very different perspective from this one is Raimundo Pannikar, *Worship and Secular Man* (New York: Orbis Books, 1973).

2. Douglas, *Symbols*, p. 20.

3. *Ibid.*, p. 25.

4. *Ibid.*, pp. 59f.

5. *Ibid.*, p. 22.

6. Cf. Johan Huizinga, *Homo Ludens* (Boston: Beacon Press, 1955).

7. James White, *New Forms of Worship* (Nashville: Abingdon, 1971), p. 51.

8. Josef Pieper, *In Tune with the World*, tr. Richard and Clara Winston (Chicago: Franciscan Herald Press, 1973), p. 27.

9. *Ibid.*, p. 21.

10. Ernest Koenker, *Secular Salvation* (Philadelphia: Fortress Press), 1965.

11. Pieper, *Tune*, p. 51.

12. A. G. Hebert, *Liturgy and Society* (London: Faber and Faber, 1935), p. 193.

13. *Aufzeichnengen aus dem Jahren 1875/79*, Gesammelte Werke (Munich: Musarion-Ausgabe, 1960), vol. 9, p. 480; quoted in Pieper, *Tune*, p. 10.

14. *Sermo* 227, quoted in Hebert, *Liturgy*, p. 85.

15. *The Parish Eucharist* (Madison: Associated Parishes, 1955), p. 4.

16. *Constitution on the Sacred Liturgy* (Collegeville, Liturgical Press, 1963), par. 2.

17. "A Letter from Romano Guardini," Herder Correspondence (August 1964), p. 239.

18. A recent positive assessment of the work of Guéranger is R. W. Franklin, "Guéranger: A View on the Centenary of His Death," *Worship* 49 (1975), pp. 318-328. A more critical view is in Louis Bouyer, *Liturgical Piety* (Notre Dame: University of Notre Dame Press, 1955), pp. 10-14, 56-58.

19. Franklin, "Guéranger," p. 328.

20. Bouyer, *Piety*, p. 58.

21. *Ibid.*, pp. 59f.

22. An excellent history of the Roman Catholic aspect of the movement is Ernest Koenker, *The Liturgical Renaissance in the Roman Catholic Church* (St. Louis: Concordia, 1966). Two other studies, both in Massey H. Shepherd (ed.) *The Liturgical Renewal of the Chuch* (New York: Oxford, 1960), are Shepherd, "The History of the Liturgical Renewal," pp. 21-52 and Arthur Carl Piepkorn, "The Protestant Worship Revival and the Lutheran Liturgical Movement," pp. 54-97.

23. Charles Davis, "Odo Casel and the Theology of Mysteries," *Worship* 34 (1960), p. 432.

24. *Constitution*, par. 24.

25. *Ibid.*, par. 14.

26. Frank S. Cellier, *Liturgy Is Mission* (New York: Seabury, 1964), pp. 21f.

27. For a discussion of liturgical reform, see my *Liturgical Change: How Much Do We Need?* (New York: Seabury, 1975).

28. Douglas, *Symbols*, pp. 27f.

29. Marshall McLuhan, *The Gutenberg Galaxy* (Toronto: University of Toronto Press, 1962), pp. 137f, 141.

30. An interesting discussion of the implications for worship of ocular and oral cultures is Clarence Rivers, "We're Going to Have a Good Time!" *Liturgy* 21.3 (March 1976), pp. 68-77.

31. Micks, *Future*, p. 176.

32. *Ibid.*, p. 178.

33. *Constitution*, par. 21.
34. *Ibid.*, par. 38.
35. Rivers, "Good Time," p. 77.
36. Pieper, *Tune*, p. 32.
37. *Ibid.*, p. 22.